blue
rider
press

THE
LOST
CHAPTERS

Also by Leslie Schwartz

Angels Crest

Jumping the Green

THE LOST CHAPTERS

Finding Recovery and
Renewal One Book at a Time

LESLIE SCHWARTZ

BLUE RIDER PRESS
New York

blue
rider
press

An imprint of Penguin Random House LLC
375 Hudson Street
New York, New York 10014

Photograph on page vii courtesy Jan Burns
The verse quoted in the dedication is from Jack Gilbert's "A Brief for the Defense."
The poem on pages 29–30 is from *Twelve Moons* by Mary Oliver. Copyright ©
1972, 1973, 1974, 1976, 1977, 1978, 1979 by Mary Oliver. Reprinted with the
permission of Little, Brown and Company. All rights reserved.

ISBN 9780525534631
Ebook ISBN 9780525534648

Printed in the United States of America
10 9 8 7 6 5 4 3 2 1

Book design by Cassandra Garruzzo

For my family,
"We stand at the prow again of a small ship . . ."
&
for beautiful Qaneak

CONTENTS

THE
LOST
CHAPTERS

BOOKLIST

IN ALPHABETICAL ORDER BY
AUTHOR'S LAST NAME

AA in Prison

The Big Book of Alcoholics Anonymous

I Know Why the Caged Bird Sings—Maya Angelou

Maggie and Me—Damian Barr

A History of Loneliness—John Boyne

The Night of the Gun—David Carr

When Things Fall Apart—Pema Chödrön

The House on Mango Street—Sandra Cisneros

A Tale of Two Cities—Charles Dickens

All the Light We Cannot See—Anthony Doerr

The Gathering—Anne Enright

Unbroken—Laura Hillenbrand

The Woman Warrior—Maxine Hong Kingston

One Hundred Years of Solitude—Gabriel García
   Márquez

Notes from the Song of Life—Tolbert McCarroll

The Children Act—Ian McEwan

New and Selected Poems, Volume One—Mary Oliver

A Tale for the Time Being—Ruth Ozeki

Dear Committee Members—Julie Schumacher

My Life as a Foreign Country—Brian Turner

Beautiful Ruins—Jess Walter

Ethan Frome—Edith Wharton

Prologue

One day, as I was crawling along the 10 Freeway heading to Santa Monica, I heard an amazing story on the radio. In 1980, a thirty-one-year-old Somali man, Mohamed Barud, wrote a letter complaining about the appalling conditions of his local hospital. At that time, Somalia was ruled by a military dictator named Siad Barre. When Barre's government saw the letter, Barud was sentenced to life in prison. His charge: treason. He was arrested and incarcerated three months after his wedding to his beloved partner, Ismahan. Like countless others, Barud was sentenced to prison for his words.

While in prison, Barud was not allowed to speak to anyone. He paced his tiny cell all day and night, feeling like he was losing his mind. Aware that the government was pressuring the spouses of the imprisoned to divorce their husbands, Barud began to imagine his wife out there making love to other men, enjoying life to the fullest. The urge to kill himself presented itself with a force he never could have imagined, and soon the nightmares came: that he would attempt suicide, and at the last moment of consciousness, he'd realize he'd made a mistake.

Then one day, he heard a tap on the wall. It was from another prisoner in the cell next to him, Dr. Adan Abokor. Abokor was a doctor who worked at the hospital that Barud had complained about. Abokor, knowing that Barud was probably losing his mind, taught him the alphabet as a series of knocks and claps on the wall.

"I was trying to counsel him," Abokor said. "I explained to him through the wall that he's not going to go mad and he's not going to die."

So they began to talk, by knocks and claps. The letter "A" equaled one tap, "B," two, and so on. Then one day as Abokor was getting a change of clothes, his first in two years, a guard transporting him back to his cell gave him a book. Abokor began to read that book to Barud through the wall. The book? *Anna Karenina*. Eight hundred pages, 350,000 words, two million letters, knocked and clapped into Barud's ears one letter at a time.

It was that book that allowed Barud to find his salvation. He began to see, through the character of Anna, that not only was he suffering but so, too, was his wife.

"It helped me to survive," Barud said. "You realize you cannot concentrate on yourself. Then you realize, I'm not alone in this very difficult situation."

After eight years, Barud was freed into a different Somalia than the one under which he'd been imprisoned, a country now torn apart by civil war. He found Ismahan in a refugee camp. Despite the government's pressure to divorce her husband, her resolve to stay married won out, and they are still married to this day. Barud says the book, and the act of Akobar reading it to him, saved not only his life but the love he had for Ismahan.

On January 12, 2014, I was sentenced to ninety days in Century Regional Detention Facility—Los Angeles County jail—for charges relating to driving drunk. I'd committed my offenses while in a 414-day relapse from double-digit years of sobriety. During that year and seven weeks, I was in a chronic state of blackout. I had fallen so profoundly into the mental illness that accompanies alcoholism that I was no longer able to work. I lost every job I had as a freelance writer and writing teacher. My family eventually moved away. My friends, no longer able to help me, left. I was totally alone. Even the dog was scared of me. She hid in the closet while I stumbled through the empty house.

I can only explain my decision to drink again in this way: I had found myself stuck in sobriety. My spirit felt dry and depressed. I couldn't see any way out of a sense of confusion and unhappiness that had come on when I turned fifty. There weren't any crises, there wasn't any one reason; I was just sad, isolated, and lonely. So I drank. That's what alcoholics without a solution do. You could say that one drink led me all the way to Century Regional, known in the vernacular as Lynwood. Of those ninety days, I would serve half the time, minus eight days for time served previously as per California's sentencing laws. Thirty-seven days.

Obviously, compared to Barud, and the countless number of human beings in jails and prisons throughout the world, I did only a breath of time and, unlike Barud, I had committed a real crime. But incarceration isn't even appropriate for animals. The experience of being caged was soul crushing. Some days the shame and loneliness I felt was so bad I'd have to check out mentally. By the time I had accepted a plea bargain, I was six months sober, something people usually celebrate, but my experience, which was colored by the inequitable outcomes of a broken and corrupt criminal system, put a daily weight on that hard-won sobriety. I was finished with drugs and alcohol, but like Barud I hadn't yet ruled out the thought of taking my own life.

Living through this experience exposed me to new levels of human cruelty. During my time, I saw ghastly things. I saw deputies fuck women in the Dayroom bathroom in exchange for drugs, so imperious they made little effort to hide it. (On September 14, 2017, a ten-year veteran of the LA County Sheriff's Department named Giancarlo Scotti was arrested for "oral copulation" and "rape under color of authority" at Lynwood. There are so many more like him who will never be arrested.) I saw women being beaten for keeping extra hair ties in their cells. I saw women who'd been raped in the streets being forced to suffer the lingering hands of male guards "searching them" for contraband in their bras and crotches. One day I saw a deputy, pissed off for no apparent reason, take away a woman's court-sanctioned extra mattress. She had a disability. "You're a fat slob," he told her. "You don't need this, you need to get off your fat ass."

I watched countless times as human beings failed us in jail, over and over again, with shattering cruelty. But like Barud, it was literature that saved me. The books that I had requested from family and friends and that arrived new from the bookstore every week were the balm to my endless hurt. Those precious stories, priceless gifts, restored me. They brought me back from the shock and hopelessness I'd experienced from my massive case of self-destruction and the grim consequences that followed.

In jail, I was allowed to receive three books a week from the outside. Over the course of my six weeks of incarceration, I managed to receive twenty-one books, three over the limit, which gives me some satisfaction. I love that three extra books, which might have earned me a stay in the hole, got past those sadistic guards who scorned the rules themselves when they opened our mail and arbitrarily decided whether we would get it on any given day. Often I would see my books sitting on the deputy's counter for days, as if to taunt me. There was no measure to the fury and impotence I felt at being tortured like that.

All told, between the books sent to me by friends and family, and those I read that were left behind by other inmates, I read about a book a day during my incarceration. I have always been a voracious reader, but my lapse from sobriety had extinguished that side of me. My experience at Lynwood reignited my love for books in a way that was visceral, elemental. While reading, I was able to forget, for just a little while, the shame I had about destroying my life by taking that one drink. They united me with people. One such book brought me to the person who changed my life forever. Two books in particular forged a friendship that shouldn't have happened and wouldn't have anywhere else on Earth. Another eased me into myself, then pushed me away from myself so that I found my freedom. Not all the books I received had a lasting impact on me or changed my perceptions of my life and the awfulness of my situation. But a surprising number not only enlightened me, they transformed me in ways that would permanently change me.

Strangely, too, each one of those books that reconstructed my worldview, magically, *coincidentally*, arrived unbidden, at precisely the moment I needed it. It was as if a wizard conducted the exact delivery of each book so that it exactly matched the challenge I was currently experiencing. Like Barud, who learned from *Anna Karenina* that in love, there is suffering, each book I received had a destiny. Each taught me what I needed to learn at the moment, most especially when it came to rising above the challenges and cruelty of county jail. Without them, I may have fallen apart, and I surely would have left there a lesser person.

From the books I read in jail, a slow hope began to grow. I started to yearn for something new—a different kind of life, one less concerned with outside appearances and the backwash left by my giant ego. The characters in my books had found humility, I reasoned, so why couldn't I? I thirsted for freedom, not from jail—that would come soon enough—but in a more expansive way, from myself. And what I wanted more than anything else was an ordinary god, one that had nothing to do with religion. Books could give me that wisdom and show me the way out of darkness.

One day, during my incarceration, I remembered a particularly devastating moment in my childhood. My parents, feuding again while drunk, upended the dinner table one night, and while dishes flew and broke, my mom and dad raged like twin tempests around my brothers and me. My youngest brother and I fled for the hall closet, my hiding place that I'd outfitted with scores of candy, books, and a flashlight. I used that hideout many times. I followed my brother in, but not before grabbing a book called *The Little House*. Written by Virginia Lee Burton, the Caldecott Medal–winning book was about a house with a sweet face made of windows and a door. Eventually the house was abandoned while the city grew up around it. All the noise and pollution destroyed the spirit of that house until, one day, a new family fell in love with it and moved it to the country. I read it to my brother there, in the closet, with the flashlight, and I believed for the both of us that in time we would find that house, that everything would be all right.

In Lynwood, a place known for people doing the hardest time anyone will ever do in the state of California, including in comparison to state prison, I held on to my books with white knuckles. Sometimes it felt like I turned the pages with the power of sheer sadness alone. Other times, with joy. And over the days I spent there, I was softened, the way my brother and I had been eased by the spirit of hope that resides in the pages of every great book. What I found there, in that place, as I shared my books and my fellow inmates shared theirs with me, was a disposition of boundless humanity among the incarcerated women there. The biggest miracle, of course, is that I found a way to forgive myself for the pain and suffering I had ushered into the lives of the people who loved me. As much as anything else, I credit stories for that; for making me feel whole in a place where the carcasses of addiction were so evident, and the temptation to otherwise return to the old life of an addict was suspended each day, one word at a time.

CHAPTER ONE

Processing In

Day two of processing in. I have not yet had anything to drink or eat. We stand there—a line of twelve women—in a freezing open warehouse that is so huge you could put a volleyball court inside of it. We are nude while deputies with guns order us to squat and cough while they shine flashlights up our asses and vaginas. The woman next to me, probably in her forties, is on her period.

"I'm bleeding," she says. She is crying softly.

"Shut up and squat," her deputy says.

I watch her menstrual blood flow to the floor.

A rabbi who I spoke to for comfort in the days leading up to my surrender to Century Regional Detention Facility said, "They can take your clothes, but they can't take your dignity."

He was wrong.

I know this now as I comply with orders in this barnlike structure. It is intolerably cold and dark and cavernous. I am not afraid. I am outraged.

After they shine their flashlight up me, hands on their guns, then order me to give up my clothes and put their plastic underwear and size triple-X blues on, the God I think I know is incinerated. A rogue hatred settles into my spirit and makes a rat's nest of that small part of me where I store such things. Even in the years to come, I cannot release the memory of such indignity, the exposure of my most private body, under threat of gun and billy club, to people who collect a paycheck for probing me there.

There is a reason people use the cattle metaphor when speaking about jails. When I am dressed in my blues and shoes two sizes too large for me, I am marched back with the others, *again*, into the holding cell. Except when in the strip-search area, I have been in this holding cell for nearly two days, stuffed full of women sitting on the urine-soaked floor. The cell is packed. There must be a hundred of us shoved into a space the size of a garden shed. The other three "holding" cells are also exploding with bodies, so many that the barred doors—throwback to an earlier time before steel firewalled doors—cannot be locked. I still have not eaten. I have not had a drink. I don't know what time it is. The clock on the wall is stuck at 2:37.

Hours pass by, each minute an entire anthem to human depravity. At one point, a young woman scowls at a huge, butchy guard. The guard tells her, "Wipe that off your face." The young woman says, "Fuck you." It happens so fast—she is dragged from the holding cell and handcuffed. She kicks out, flailing, and is tased and hauled away. I have seen people discard trash with more sensitivity. In that moment, the memory of my last arrest, the violence of it, comes to the surface. I am momentarily unable to breathe as I shove it down and away, to be dealt with later.

While in holding, one woman braids my hair for me. She is very thin and frail. Another offers to trade shoes. Hers are too small for her, but they fit me perfectly. A third offers me a spot on the bench, moving over to make room for my tiny body. In jail, where overcrowding is the norm, it pays to be small. When lukewarm milk and plastic-wrapped meat-product burritos arrive, my stomach turns. I give mine to the prostitute next to me.

I am almost six months' clean and sober and I spend the time in holding staring in amazement at the junkies and prostitutes, thinking about how I got here. It is not easy, because due to the blackout all I remember of it is the beating I took at the hands of LAPD—a relentless memory that invades my thinking with a stubborn regularity, like a drumbeat that never stops. For 414 days until, miraculously, I stopped drinking and using, I lived in a state of chronic blackout. According to neuroscientists, the alcohol- and drug-induced blackout is not simply a case of memory loss. People who suffer from blackouts never retrieve their memories because there are no memories to retrieve. The mind-altering substances in high doses interfere with the way the brain processes and makes memories. In a blackout, because of the drugs and/or alcohol, no memories are ever recorded by the brain. It is as if your life never happened.

This would not be true for the people I most damaged by my drinking and using. They remembered everything.

As I sit there, waiting, waiting, waiting to be processed, I try to hold onto the thought that at least I am sober. I am sober as they pull me out of the cell to take my mug shot. It will be my fourth one and, I know, my last. I understood then, after having my photo taken by police over and over again, why in some cultures it is believed that photographs steal your soul. After that, they fit my wrist with a band. It looks like an industrial-grade hospital band, but it is secured with unbreakable grommets. The deputy puts it on too tight. I am skin and bones, and it rubs my wrist, already torn and scarred by handcuffs, raw and bloody. The wristband contains my name and booking number and a barcode. I don't know what the barcode is for until one day in my last module one of the deputies scans it with a handheld device and every piece of information you could ever want about me—age, criminal charges, release dates, etc.—pops up on his small portable screen.

To know that my identity has been reduced to a wristband pains me. I struggle against losing my freedom, against having these twenty-two-year-old deputies lord over me, as if I am nothing. They send me back to holding and now there are even more of us. It must be Saturday night, though who could tell? Time itself no longer exists. Only *thoughts* of time are alive. The time I am wasting is the most painful rumination; it haunts me. The time I am away from my husband and daughter is an unbearable notion. The time I am not writing or gardening. All these thoughts, yet I cannot gain a perspective of time. As Augustine of Hippo said, some sixteen hundred years ago about time, "If no one asks me, I know what it is. If I wish to explain it to him who asks, I do not know."

I just know it must be later now, the animal hours of a Saturday night. The women seem drunker. Some are clearly tweaking. More prostitutes have arrived. It is a sea of black and brown faces. The white women are few and far between, maybe one or two who look like me. Housewives, college graduates, people who live near fancy coffee shops and wear Lululemon. When we catch each other's eyes, we turn away, as if we know each other and are embarrassed to be caught seen in this place. Some of the women sleep sitting up. I can't. I am pretty sure I won't sleep for the next six weeks.

A few hours later, I am told to line up—for what, I don't know. After about half an hour of standing there, I am ushered into a room where they take my X-ray. They are looking for TB. It is clear the technician hates being there. He just wants to go home.

"Hurry up," he says to each and every one of us when he is done. "I don't have all day."

After about another hour—maybe five, though without clocks, it is difficult to tell—they finally call me. I am not a name anymore, but a number: 4261531. I am moving out of processing and into medical, the next step on the way to permanent housing. I line up with about twenty other women. Jail is confinement, but when it's not confinement, it's lining up along red stripes on the ground and then walking along the green line to the next place. They march us to a large bin where inmates in jail clothes different from the rest of us hand us our bedding. I learn these inmates are trustees who "work" in the modules. Our bedding consists of a thin, torn blanket. Rolled up inside I am supposed to find a sheet, a nightgown, thermals, and men's tube socks. I don't. There are no pillows and no pillowcases. No one gets those.

Holding my roll-up, I wait in line. Again. For god knows how long. Time has changed since I've been in here. It has slowed so far down it feels as if it's stopped. What is my daughter doing now? My husband? My best friend, Anadel? Is anyone walking the dog? Is it daylight? Or is it dark? Einstein's famous line comes to mind: "The distinction between past, present, and future is only a stubbornly persistent illusion." This has never been truer. The now that I live in isn't anything like the now that my beloveds occupy. Theirs is different space. Time, as Einstein showed us, is relative. If my family and friends are locked into my experience by their empathy, the now they experience is swifter, kinder, freer. And what they experience of time, they do so wearing their own underwear.

⌘

Finally after another hour of standing, roll-up in arms, we are marched to medical. I do not know yet that in the thirty-seven days I will spend here out of my ninety-day sentence, once I am in "permanent housing" I will actually be moved five times. Movement is essential for control. It disrupts. It causes anxiety and fear. It limits the chances for friendships and alliances.

As I stand in medical, waiting to process to my first locked cell, I remember one piece of advice a nun I had spoken to gave me. She was the former chaplain at Lynwood, and someone I knew gave me her number.

"Take the bottom bunk if you can. The jail is colder than a meat locker. The top bunk is coldest."

The icy refrigerator that is jail has lodged into the sinews of my 104-pound body. When I am assigned a cell, I make a fast walk of it for the bottom bunk, heeding the nun's advice. The bunkie I will share this five-by-ten locked concrete cell with is right behind me. I can feel her breath. She, too, is racing for the bottom bunk. I get there first and claim the lower, warmer metal plank of the bed. But immediately I feel terrible that I have won this small victory because it comes at a cost to her. I lie there, guilty.

My bunkie is a beautiful twenty-year-old heroin addict who is kicking. Almost immediately she is shitting and throwing up. I am not upset by this. I have been there. I understand. I blame my addiction partly on my empathy, because empathy hurts. I always viewed my tenderness with unfriendliness. All my life, even as a kid, especially as a kid, I'd felt broken by a sixth sense that the world was hard, that people and animals suffered needlessly, that base human nature tended toward cruelty. My empathy seemed innate, as true to me as the color of my eyes. It was a total liability in life. Until I started really drinking and using drugs, I wasn't capable of the toughness it seemed you needed to stay alive, to compete and win, win, win. My skin felt perennially inside out. But once I could hide out behind substances, I found merciful release. Only then was it easier not to care about other people, to play games and get along. But strangely, in jail I will learn that empathy is my greatest asset.

Melissa and I are exactly the same height and weight and coincidentally live in the same neighborhood "on the outs." She is second-generation Cuban, thirty-three years younger than me. I will be the minority in jail, both because I am white and because I am older.

As I lie on my metal slab, shivering, I pray even though at this point I have no faith. Prayer is habit, from an earlier time, before God vanished during strip search. *Please show me that this gets better. Please.* All I can see is the halo of those horrible orange jail lights shining grimly outside on the concrete building. At least the lights tell me it is night—but of what day, I no longer know. I have never felt more alone, more devastated in my entire life. Never before. Never after. Not even in the worst part of my addiction, when I was isolated and dying, did I feel this alone.

Both Melissa and I are shivering. She has the added burden of being dope sick. She has to get up repeatedly and vomit. Between these episodes we talk. I am needy. To feel real, I must talk to someone. Anyone. I would have talked to Vlad the Impaler if he were my bunkie. "What is it about the quality of blood you most admire?" I might have asked.

"Are you an addict?" she asks.

"Six months clean and sober," I say. I feel the unblunted cut of this sobriety as if I am being eviscerated from the inside out. Everything is too bright, too loud, too frightening, yet I am determined to walk through this without drugs or alcohol. Before, I would have picked up over a broken shoelace.

"I'm sorry for the . . ." She points to the toilet, where she has just had diarrhea.

"Oh no . . . I've been there . . ."

"Yeah," she says. It is hard not to hear a world in that word. Longing. Regret.

She is the sweetest woman with the tiniest voice. She is soft-spoken in a way that makes me think she had long ago learned not to make too much space for herself in the world. I need to keep talking to her, to alleviate the bleak sense of isolation. She tells me she is here on a warrant, that she hopes to go to court the next day and be released. She prays that they don't make her spend the weekend in jail before she can see the judge. We both know they will.

We are silent for a long time. Then I break the silence.

"I'm afraid they will call you first and I will be alone."

"Don't be afraid," she says. Years later, I still hear her voice exactly as it was.

But the fear of being alone with my thoughts is unshakeable and will follow me throughout my incarceration. The loneliness is palpable. A center-in-your-stomach loneliness, a motherless loneliness, one made worse because like all of me, it, too, is shackled. It can't take a walk. It can't be soothed by love. It is there to fend for itself.

I lie on my back on the one-inch-thick plastic mattress and gaze through the tiny window at the orange lights shining in the mist over the concrete exterior of the jail. I have never seen anything as depressing. It is as if despair built the walls of this place. My back burns with pain. Six months before my incarceration, after my last arrest in which I was charged with DUI, driving on a suspended license, and resisting arrest, I woke up in a rehab in New Mexico with the imprint of my arresting officer's boot on my back. My wrists were bloodied from the handcuffs, there was a bruise on my right cheek, my lip was swollen. They beat me after I'd made the mistake of fighting the handcuffs, yelling at them, telling them to go fuck themselves.

It was initially a DUI arrest, but later, the prosecutor decided to change the resisting-arrest charge and bump it up to battery of an officer. I had heard about this LAPD strategy: when they beat you up, law enforcement charges *you* with battery, hoping, I guess, you are dissuaded from filing suit. Before it happened to me, I always thought it was a paranoid idea, a conspiracy theory, a way to shunt the blame. I now see how naive I was. When you obey laws, as I had done for more than fifty years until my relapse, you have no idea what really goes on. There were a lot of things I didn't think were true. Now I know the truth. And believe me, it is a painful awakening.

Of course I didn't sue them. I was afraid of them. Any time I thought about that night, my breathing would be caught short, my heart would race, and that spot on my back would pulse, as if it had been lit on fire. I was a hundred pounds soaking wet at the time of my arrest, in handcuffs, in the back of a police cruiser, thrown there after I'd called the officers names and blamed them for arresting me. This was scandalous crazy-lady behavior; I take and hold that responsibility. But those officers were six foot one, about 250 pounds each, which would mean that if it were true that I had "battered" them, I would have miraculously "battered" 500 pounds and twelve feet of men carrying guns and tasers from the back seat of a police car, while handcuffed. They lied and I didn't have the heart to stand up for myself. I took their plea. Both my husband, Greg, and I, and even my attorney who said as much, understood that they add charges because they can. They know for most of us the thought of a trial is nauseating and repulsive. They know we are terrified. We submit. We just want it to end.

Now as I lie there, the battery charge is like a boil on that spot where he stepped on me, lanced and painful and bloody. It is this, not the time for DUI and driving while suspended, that makes me wish I were dead. The thought crosses my mind that even if I had battered them, driving while intoxicated was a far worse crime. I find little consolation in the fact that God saw fit to keep people out of my way. Maybe the battery charge was some karmic trade-off for the heinousness of driving drunk, but the dereliction and wrongness of it causes me so much grief. As I lie there, I am polluted by regret and rage. I can't imagine how I will live in a cage for thirty-seven days while my friends and family, depressed and anxious, wait for me to come home safely. One thing I know now: it is not the other inmates I need to fear. It is the uniforms.

Astonishingly, in that moment when I really wonder if I will be able to live one more second, I hear Melissa. Her sweet, tender voice calls out to me: "Can I come down and get under the covers with you?" I hear her fear of my possible rejection as she asks. "I'm so cold. I'll put my head at your feet. I'm just so cold and sick and scared."

I need no convincing. My relief is so intense that it feels like air filling up inside me. Such intimacy is against the rules—and I suspect such an act of kinship, too—but we are two small, lost people in a cold place, so I say yes. And it is like I've just averted death, as if a piano falling from the sky just landed an inch to the left of me.

She crawls in beside me, and with the presence of another human being, my suffering is lifted enough that I am warm and not wishing for death for the first time in days. I sleep. She does, too. Her body next to mine; between us, our shared sadness. But there is also something else. Something I don't recognize. It is impossible to name it because the word "hope" can't find its way through this morass of pain. But it is there, small and white, and it will grow.

What feels like a moment later, they call my name and send me out to whatever next hellish place I'm headed. I never see her again. Yet, for that brief moment when Melissa was asleep beside me, I understood what "holy" meant. I didn't really comprehend, until a long time later and far removed from that place, that the God who I believed had abandoned me was still there and was not only answering my prayers but saying them for me, too.

We line up again. Behind me is Shondra, a woman with whom I spent three hours outside the jail while we waited to be called in to start serving our sentences. It was a gift, her presence then. We laughed nervously together about the craziness of making us *wait* to serve time. The absurdity of us sticking around. She was beautiful, with smooth black skin, a convivial and animated woman, the perfect person to be with while you waited hours for your incarceration to start. She was sentenced to two weeks for not paying her parking tickets. Because she couldn't afford to pay, like indentured servants of the Chesapeake Colonies and former slaves, she had to do time. She was five months' pregnant with her first child. She only had parking tickets. For at least two reasons, I tell myself, I deserved to be here. But really, what wrong did she do? Be poor?

Now, days later, I see how bedraggled she looks. Her hair is tangled and messy. I must have looked as bad. We know better than to say a word to each other. It is here that I learn how to say entire sentences with my eyes. She speaks back to me with hers. Our shared shock and outrage is clear. We wait for at least another hour, standing there, holding our roll-ups. I can't imagine what it must be like to stand like that, holding linens, knowing it is your poverty that enslaves you here, all while carrying a child.

All of this standing around doing nothing gives me ample time to think about what happened, over and over and over again. And then some more. I suspect this waiting around, this standing around, this slowing down of clocks, is by design. No one likes to wait, but waiting to be locked up, not knowing what comes next *for hours,* is perfect torture.

I think. I think and think. I think more. I remember when I came out of it, not knowing what the hell had happened. There were some things I remembered; that moment especially in the cruiser before I was transported to city jail when the officer turned around and karate chopped me in the neck because I was crying too loudly. I don't remember much after that because his maneuver caused me to pass out. But I do remember coming to and hearing the other one say, "Shouldn't we check on her? She's been quiet for a long time."

For the most part, though, I didn't know the details of what I had done during that year-plus. Those days appeared to me as ghost days, inhabited by phantoms and shadows. I knew I'd lost pretty much everything that mattered to me. I chased my family away. I destroyed my career. I nearly died twice from an overdose of liquor and pills. The second, more serious time I was in the ICU, I was placed on a telemetry ward at risk for "hypotensive crisis" (dangerously low blood pressure). There were two 5150 psych holds. I was arrested four times, mostly for driving-related offenses. My license was revoked for two years. I went to seven detoxes and rehabs. I crashed two cars and lost most of my money. All that damage in just a year and forty-nine days.

I had never been in trouble with the law before. I couldn't even remember the last time I'd had a parking ticket. Maybe this was why my judge was considerate and humane to me. The judge saw my half a century of civil behavior. He saw that I was a person who, until this strange blip on the radar screen of my life, lived in concert with the laws of my community.

I believe, to this day, that out of all of them, including my own attorney, my judge was the only one who understood the Jekyll and Hyde of addiction. Among his many kindnesses, he allowed me six weeks from the time of sentencing to compliance because I was working on a book project with a deadline. He also, I realized later, did not command me to turn myself in in court and be transported in handcuffs on a sheriff's bus like most people. I voluntarily complied at the jail. This was a reprieve I appreciated only later. I'd heard the horrors of that particular ride: men in chains and locked in cages in the back, women in the front handcuffed to seats, ogled, harassed by them. Lascivious laughter at the woman's expense, the words "fuck" and "pussy" and "suck" filtering up to them.

The six weeks before my incarceration began were torture, though. I stopped eating. I barely slept. I spent the days with friends who did not leave my side. At home, my family and I were quiet, in collective shock. One day, my friend Horace and I got tattoos. I had a wedding ring inked on my ring finger because I knew I couldn't wear my diamond ring or wedding band in jail.

For Greg and my daughter, the pain was visible. It hovered over them. It was a different kind of pain when I went to jail than when I was active in my addiction. It was fear, of course, but it seemed hopeful, too. I was staying sober through the worst of things. If jail was what it would take to get on with my life, then so be it. They watched me carefully and later with a kind of pride, how I carried the weight of those charges, both true and untrue. They saw that I rose every day while I waited for my compliance date and walked through my life, determined. These were parts of me they didn't see when I was under the lock and key of my addiction.

"It was rolling chaos spreading out into all these directions," Greg said one day early on after the run had ended. I remember I was standing in the kitchen, talking endlessly about how hard my life was. He looked at me. "Are you serious?" he said. "Do you have any idea what you did to us?"

I grew quiet.

"I don't really want to hear about how much it hurts *you*," he said.

He was right. I never spoke about what happened from that standpoint of extreme self-centeredness again.

My daughter was more blunt. "Sometimes I would look at you when you were drunk and wish you were dead."

I remember very little from the sentencing. I was in shock. It took me almost a year to understand the gravity of what I had done because the perceived overprosecution removed me from myself and embittered me. I couldn't see over that visor of anger and self-pity for a long time. I remember at the time the grief on my husband's face, the woe and speechlessness as he held my hand on that hard bench outside Part 45 of the LA County criminal courts building.

"This is so messed up," he said. "This is so wrong." I could feel it through his skin, how sad and bewildered he was. His love for me, so steadfast and gorgeous, pained me. All I could think was how much I had hurt him, my family, and the friends who loved me.

During that six-week interval between sentencing and incarceration, I felt like I was not really alive. It was as if I were floating above the earth, but only by six inches so the harshness of my reality could be endured, but from a distance. I read the newspaper every day, and every day I found a preponderance of local crime and sentencing stories; the kind of stories that never really interested me before. I would read about other people who had done so much more mayhem than I had and received shorter sentences. They were all men. I remember once reading about a college kid from Glendale, California, who had sexually assaulted two women, an act that would forever alter the lives of his victims. He received the same sentence as I did. He was out before I surrendered; in thirty days—seven days less than I would serve even though I had not assaulted anyone with my hands. Only my words.

It took me a long time—a very long time—to forgive the cops who beat me up, those men with guns who towered over me, but eventually I was able to. It happened in a flash one day some two years later. Somehow, I fully comprehended their own fear, their exhaustion, and the lack of services they received to deal with crazy people like me. I saw their humanness. Forgetting their harms, I looked to where I was wrong, and contacted them both so that I could apologize for being in the center of that night. They never responded. At the time, I understood why and I forgave them again. But that was a long time coming. Now, as I stood in line waiting to be transferred to the next place in jail, I only wanted them dead. *Fuckers*, I thought. Facing me would be facing what they did to me. Their silence had only revealed their cowardice.

All of sudden, a deputy shouted, "Let's go, ladies. Hurry up."

Shondra and I exchanged glances.

The deputy knocked me on the shoulder. "Keep your eyes forward."

That touch burned. I wanted to tell him to go fuck himself. To keep his disgusting hands off my body. That they all wore gloves, like we were feces, incensed me. I remembered—was it a day ago, two days now?—when Greg drove me to Lynwood, how bleak the city looked, the endless traffic on the freeway, the low-rises, the smokestacks burning toxins into the air, the Section 8 housing. I thought about the way the poor were shunted off into the wilderness of projects to live by freeways and chemical plants, next to prisons and jails. I remembered Greg kissing me good-bye, the heartbreak in his eyes. I knew that I must live under the counsel of a higher authority, something bigger, more divine and more principled than my drunk self, the cops and lawyers who put me there. On some level, I knew that peace would come only when I stopped doubting the justice of God's ways. The problem was, that authority felt gone and wasted. Self-pity and bitterness had erased my faith.

Yet I knew intuitively that I should not take to heart the misguided belief of those in the system that it was they who held sway over me, that by virtue of their robes and suits they were somehow better than me. I didn't think that. I still don't. What I can remember now is that I had to hold onto Greg's love, my daughter's faith in me, and the friends who had pledged to stand by me forever. Their incredible love and devotion was the biggest god I could manage then. And this: I had to hold onto that something; the kernel within that told me—*which I knew was the undeniably lawful and just truth*—that I was good. That I was worthy. That I was not the measure of my addiction. I understood that this information, however softly spoken, came from within myself, and that if I was still and listened hard enough, maybe one day I could be restored and redeemed to myself, to the people who loved me and stood by me, and to the people of my community, whose lives I had risked by my mistakes. But I couldn't put any kind of god in that equation. Not now in this place. I was finished with that bullshit.

CHAPTER TWO

Pregnant Module

The litter under the tree
Where the owl eats—shrapnel

Of rat bones, gull debris—
Sinks into the wet leaves

Where time sits with her slow spoon,
Where we becomes singular, and a quickening

From light-years away
Saves and maintains. O holy

Protein, o hallowed lime,
O precious clay!

Tossed under the tree
The cracked bones

Of the owl's most recent feast
Lean like shipwreck, starting

The long fall back to the center—
The seepage, the flowing,

The equity: sooner or later
In the shimmering leaves

The rat will learn to fly, the owl
Will be devoured.
—Mary Oliver, "Bone Poem," *New and Selected Poems*

I am eventually sent to permanent housing. "Permanent housing" is a euphemism. More essentially, it means you will be permanently moving. The term "permanent" simply distinguishes it from the temporary holding cells in processing and medical where you get your five-second "checkup" from nurses and doctors who despise their jobs and you.

I am housed in Pregnant Dorm. I do not know why. At fifty-three, I am closer to being dead than bringing someone to life. But of course, it makes me think of my daughter, the months I carried her in my belly, the day of her birth, the fact that other than the 414 days of my relapse from years of sobriety, my daughter had never seen me drunk or high.

"Really," I say under my breath. *"Pregnant Dorm?"*

Having renounced the puny God I thought I once had, I still find myself turning to an *idea* of God. Only now it is an idea into which I pour all my hatred. So my arrival among incarcerated pregnant women seems meant as some kind of cosmic cruelty, a continuation of the brutality that began with the ever-widening gyre of my addiction and its consequences. Pain upon pain. Endless, ceaseless pain.

I arrive in Pregnant Dorm at 3 a.m. This is the preferred time for movement so that the other inmates don't get agitated watching new people being marched into the module. I am sent there with twelve others, including Shondra. Shondra was, like me, in a very small minority in that neither of us had been locked up before. Most people, I discovered, had served time at least once, but most often two, three, four times. Especially the prostitutes who were routinely picked up, thrown into jail, and released. An endless wheel of arrest, incarceration, arrest, incarceration. I began to think of them as the income generators for the prison industrial complex. More tax dollars.

I am assigned an upper-tier cell. Unknown to me, I am "restricted" to a bottom bunk. Because she'd asked, I told the cunty nurse in medical about a broken shoulder I'd suffered a year before while intoxicated. The cunty nurse did one thing for me that would ease my incarceration. She "restricted" me to a bottom bunk, which meant I would never have to fight for it again. I only learned about this when the deputy in Pregnant Dorm told me so.

The deputy, in the usual detached and agonizingly slow pace, dispatches us to our cells one by one. I am second to last, after Shondra. I watch Shondra disappear around some bunks in what I learn is called the Dayroom—the main floor of the jail—and into a cell. I never see her again. But Greg, who met her when he dropped me off, sees her three days later when he returns to put money on my books. She has been released. He remembers her and gives her a ride home. It is from her that he first learns about the horrors of our experience. He tells me later it eats at him. He worries about me until we are able to speak. He worries about me until he can visit. Then he worries some more.

The deputy doesn't look at me. She is busy looking at her desk, something very important there. In fact, these deputies, both men and women, are bored out of their skulls like we are, which is why they so often resort to cruelty and humiliation. It's something to do.

"Cell 41," she says.

I stand there. Where the fuck is Cell 41?

"Well, go on," she says.

"Where do I go?"

For the first time she looks at me.

"Upper tier."

"Okay. How do I get there?"

I have not had an opportunity to look around the module. I don't know where the stairs are.

"You really don't know? Have you never been here before?" she asks. Her voice is loud. The trustees to her right are staring at us. The condescension is something I will never get used to. It will keep me in a state of perpetual simmering rage.

"Well, uh, I've never been in jail before, for one," I say, telling myself, *Don't get smart, this is why you're here in the first place.*

She looks at me in disbelief.

"Serious?"

Seriously, I think. *Speak proper English, you bitch.* To be talked down to by people who barely have a high school education is one of the most humiliating experiences of my life. And to think they are the ones carrying guns. No wonder, I think, so many innocent people are dead.

"This your first time?" She laughs. Like not going to county jail is something to be ashamed of, like there will inevitably and positively be a next time. This strange twist shocks me. How can I feel embarrassed that I've never been incarcerated before? And yet, somehow I do.

"Jones, take her up," she says to one of the trustees. You can hear in her voice that I am Deputy's burden today.

A beautiful older black woman with light blue eyes walks toward me. I notice the dark circles beneath her eyes. She exudes compassion. I breathe for the first time. I am safe.

"Come on, hon," she says. "I'll take you up, baby."

She is someone's mom, someone's grandmother, someone's auntie. She becomes my silent friend and the mom I need so desperately. I will find out later Jones is fighting her case. She has been ripping Nordstrom off, to the tune of thousands. They want her to do ten years. She is hoping with the time served in Lynwood—so far almost a year—she will get probation and restitution because of her clean record. From then on, she smiles at me, and when we become friendly she will hug me and then say, every single time, "I am so tired, Leslie. So tired." Everyone calls her Miss Jones.

My bunkie is awake, waiting for me, casually eating a hard-boiled egg. She is an enormous, crazy-haired, toothless woman, with gang tats. Her name is Vanessa Rodriguez. She is El Eme, Mexican Mafia.

"Hey," she says, smiling. She has no teeth. She is obese. Yet her eyes, there's something there, a sweetness.

"Hi," I say. I am exhausted, but wired.

"First time?" she says.

I nod.

She holds out some horrible food item that she's fished out of a cup (it looks vaguely turd-like) and offers it to me.

"Oh, no thanks," I say. "But thanks."

"Here," she says, putting her cup with the corpse of food within down on the desk. "Let me show you how to make a pillow."

She does some crazy thing with my sheet and the two-inch plastic mattress so that there is a rolled-up pillow at the end. This move can only come from practice, I think. I will never figure out how to do it. Later, she will tell me she is called Duckie. Only I am allowed to call her that. And that is how I will remember her. Always. With insane love. Duckie.

Boredom. It's physical. It visits you almost immediately in jail. It is like a spore and it takes over. You grow heavier and heavier

34

from it. Very quickly every part of your body is suffused with its implacable hold over you. This boredom is mean. It tells you that you will always be there.

Before my date with Lynwood, I found out that I am allowed three books a week to be sent to me from Amazon. They must arrive unopened, with a shipping label. I am desperate for these books. My first week passes with nothing. Some days I am blank with depression, others terrified by the appetite of my yearning for what I don't have. Each day that passes without them feels as if I have spent another day un-alive.

One day, during those first dissociative days in Pregnant Dorm, I visit the so-called library during program. "Program" I learn is both a noun and a verb. The way jail is set up, inmates spend twenty-three hours a day locked in their cells. "Program" is the word they use for the one hour that the deputies let us out of our cages, but only if we've been good doggies. During program, you showered, made your calls, and if you felt like it, exercised in the fifty-square-foot patio. It wasn't outdoors, but it was close. There was a twenty-foot wall and, on top of that, two feet of razor wire that blocked access to the outside. Once, I saw a flock of seagulls drift past. Mostly, you just heard the cars from the 105 Freeway. On the patio, you had the opportunity to breathe in smog instead of jailhouse funk.

In addition to being both a noun and a verb, I am struck by the word itself: "program." Program is also a thing you do when you want to brainwash people, mold them into your lackeys or followers. Cult leaders program their recruits. Jailers program prisoners to feel worthless and forgotten. In Lynwood, they use program as a weapon. If one inmate does one thing they don't like, they shut it down for everyone. We stay locked up for twenty-four, thirty-six, forty-eight hours. Whatever. They don't care. Shift changes and the new deputy does what he or she wants. Whenever I hear the word "program," which is often, I always bristle.

On this day, I head to the "library" during program. The "library" in Pregnant Dorm consists almost exclusively of a two-tiered metal cart of Bibles, study guides for the Bible, Bible excerpts, Bible journals, Bibles in español, and AA books. It is not a separate room. It's just a pitiful shelving unit. Then, across the Dayroom, under the stairs to the upper tier, I see another metal shelving unit, an explosion of books all over the place on the floor. I've hit the motherlode. Here there are torn paperbacks—mostly romance novels with booby women on the cover and men wearing tights with bulging penises. But I see some John Grisham. There's Stephen King. I could stomach that, if I ran out of my own. Then I find Ethan Canin's collection of short stories. What the . . . ? I put it in the ginormous pocket of my gargantuan prison blues. I feel like I am stealing something.

Next to me is a small, pregnant young woman. She's African American. I try to make polite conversation with her.

"Wow, slim pickings, huh?"

She doesn't look at me and she doesn't answer. It is as if I am not there. I tell myself, *You are not here, you are not here.* Sort of like Dorothy's "There's no place like home." Only I open my eyes and I'm still there, next to a woman who won't acknowledge me because, I believe, I am white. She wanders off. I have the books to myself. It almost looks like someone donated a Santa's bag of library rejects—some even have *Los Angeles County Library* stamped on the binding. So many are torn and ratty, but others look brand-new. I notice some have the booking numbers of other inmates and realize they've been left behind. I am giddy about this overflowing shelf of goodness because of the hidden gem of Ethan Canin. *There must be more*, I think, *if I just go through it with patience.* I feel like I am searching for buried treasure. It is the first time I feel joy since I waited outside to start my sentence.

All of a sudden the pregnant woman returns. She hands me a book.

"You might like this," she says.

It's called *Esther and Ryzhy*. It's about two Jewish grandmothers who survived Stalin and the Nazis. I look up to thank the pregnant woman, but she is gone. How *weird*. The spooky thing about jail, I will find, are these small incidents that arise, as if out of smoke. Like a magic trick. She must have figured I was Jewish. I don't know how, though I suppose most people's Jewdar goes up when they look at me. Regardless, I chose to view her gift as the olive branch it was for the words she couldn't say to me. The gesture of literature—one that she took the time to think would appeal to me—was marvelous. Kinetic almost. I felt the wizardry then of books: how they unite us, how they can fill the void when words can't be spoken. I wanted to thank her, but I realized I had hardly looked at her myself. Was her unsolicitousness a reaction to my perceived rudeness? I had spent so little time looking at her that I really had no idea what she looked like. I gazed out toward the Dayroom, guilty.

I was grateful for that book, though, because I could not predict when my books would arrive. Everyone was telling me they would not get there for a month. (They were wrong about that, thank God.) Cracking it open, I begin my habit, one that will stay with me even after I'm released, of reading slowly. It is like mindful eating, where every morsel is chewed with intention to glean flavor and gratitude. How long, I wonder, have I ignored the abundance of my life, by rushing through it— eating, reading, sleeping, making love—to get to the next thing. *Go slow.* I say to myself. *Forgive yourself. Remember your blessings.*

The next Tuesday, a week or so in, three books and five letters arrive. The books are so beautiful. Dazzling. *All the Light We Cannot See. New and Selected Poems* by Mary Oliver. *The Big Book.* I pick up Mary Oliver's book. When I have it in my hands, I hold it to my chest and I feel that my heart is literally pounding with love. One of the letters I receive is from myself. In it, suspecting that I might need the words, I tell myself I am not a criminal, that there are people who love me, people who think I am brave. I asked Greg to send it to me once he had my booking number. (Inmates do not receive money or mail without booking numbers.)

Duckie is down in Dayroom in jail school when my first three books arrive. Her burping and farting and singing and grunting have left the cell, strangely, too quiet. The door stays slightly ajar, a benefit I receive while she is in school. Those two inches of air make the entire difference between claustrophobia and freedom.

I open up Mary Oliver and smell the pages. New. Like paste and rain. I lay the book for a moment open on my chest and stare at the bunk above me where someone has scrawled a quote from the Bible: "For all have sinned and fall short of the glory of God." I want to scratch that out. Over time I am able to blot it all out using the fruit stickers that come stuck on my apples and bananas. One fruit sticker at a time until it is gone. How can anyone have a god that doesn't think they are perfect exactly as they are? It seems obvious to me that a just God would *know* we are human. Even my husband doesn't pick on me for my mistakes. Why would a loving God stoop lower than him, a mere mortal?

I turn to a random page in the book. "Bone Poem." I recognize immediately that Oliver is writing about the predator and its prey, the owl and the rat. Who, she posits, is really the more powerful? It's a Hegelian construct. The slave becomes the master, the master the slave. She speaks about falling back to the center, and in a sense, she affirms the idea that things always bounce back from inequity. If you are patient enough, the poem tells us, reversals will take place; the underdog will not just triumph, but be understood.

I settle myself into that poem. It is the bed I lie in.

I ponder the way the poem speaks of the long and painful turning back to equilibrium, that place that is balanced and steady, and most of all just. When I read the words "the long fall back to the center," I wonder when that fall will begin for me. Is there even such a thing? I didn't think so then. And when would I, this rat I had become, learn to fly like the owl, as Oliver promises in the poem? It hurts to read and contemplate the hopeful notion that reckoning and readjustment always happen because, as I sit in my cell, knowing what really happened during the arrest that put me here, I do not believe this is true. I believe that the powerful always win. And I don't like that I think of myself as that rat whose bones, as Oliver writes in his poem, are eaten with relish by the majestic owl that lords over the rodent's puny life.

What is it, I wonder, about the rat—dirty, filthy, disease carrying? Is it just our revulsion of that hairless spiral of a tail, or the rat-a-tat of its claw-feet scurrying through bushes, that blinds us to the rat's ingenuity, shrewdness, and intelligence?

Mary Oliver and I have a couple of things in common. For starters, we both began writing poetry when we were fourteen. I stopped writing poems, though, and she didn't. We part company there, along with her particular genius for her craft—oh, and her Nobel, her Pulitzer, her many published books, the list goes on.

But on the earthly plain, we are also both walkers. I probably walk, on a good day, six miles. I walk on trails. I walk along the Los Angeles River. I walk around lakes. The first thing I do when I go out of town, whether it's Iowa City or Jerusalem, is find the best walking trails. I will walk anywhere. Once, in Tel Aviv, I walked eleven miles in one day, along the Mediterranean Sea, to the walled city of Jaffa, darting in and out of its ancient alleyways, then through the White City and Neve Tzedek, where the old buildings muted the sounds around me, showing me I am small and insignificant in a centuries-old world.

Oliver's stomping grounds were nature. Once, she said, she found herself walking in the woods with no pen. After that, she hid pencils in the trees so she would always be able to stop and write. Pencils in the trees—better, I think, than gold nuggets. It's ingenious. I can't count the number of times out walking somewhere when I've been inspired but had no paper, no pen. I can't use a phone, that small hell-machine. Oliver walks with a notebook, hand sewn. I do, too, when I remember to bring it, but mine is a crappy one, an artifact from the ninety-nine-cent bin at the drugstore.

In Oliver's poem "Rain," divided into seven parts, I read about myself. It is a winding poem, bleak in some places, but Mary Oliver can't help but be optimistic. It is just that sometimes she chooses the less starry-eyed map to show us our journeys. I am pulled into Part 2 because it is about incarceration and escape, at least superficially. Ultimately the poem declares that it takes courage not just to escape the literal bars of barbed wire and detention, but the deeper, more oppressive jail of poverty, disease, hunger and isolation. In the poem Oliver asks the reader to imagine what it feels like to be forced to clutch by the handful the barbed wire that surrounds you as though your life depends on it. The contemplation for me is this: Is it possible to endure physical and emotional pain even when you know the freedom on the other side isn't guaranteed?

Would it be too easy for me to hold this poem up as the ballad for my circumstances? And yet, it is just that. She is speaking of that wild country of pain. But it is more than that. In the poem she is careful to point out how it is only when we walk through that pain (or climb the fences over it) that we find abundance and joy and fearlessness. Defeat is not the end. It is, she seems to say, only the beginning. There is another freedom on the other side. Literal poverty, isolation, addiction, and incarceration are not crimes. The crime is giving up on our personal liberty. We must bleed before we find freedom.

What can I say about myself struggling against the bankruptcy of lockup and, worse, my paucity of spirit? Do I want to be sent back to the camp inside—that treacherous place where my mind wants to whisper the lies to me—that I am worthless, depraved, useless to myself and others? Or should I carry forth, mired in bog, prey to alligators and anaconda, to find as in the poem the food to sustain me, the beauty of the natural world to remind me of joy. Even wheat must be transformed into bread. It is not picked from the earth, a perfect thing, but it must endure and tolerate the transformation into its useful incarnation.

What Oliver doesn't say, but that I understand, is that the swamp on the other side of the wire that we must also cross to get to freedom is not what we think it is. The stinging nettles, skunkweed, and black widows of the swamp give way to the bald eagle, the black bear, the great blue heron. Nobility, an idea learned only in times of hardship, lives in our minds. Even if, for a long while, we cannot see past the poison oak and the hungry crocodile to the flowering dogwood, whose brilliance alights in spring, it will nevertheless always arrive. It lives within us. It blooms over and over again, despite its harsh surroundings.

In jail, I clutch the handfuls of rage, of sorrow, of despair and shame like my life depends on it.

Locked up, the past mutates. You don't think about yesterday; sameness and anomie obliterate the day before. But you think about years ago, each memory coming alive. And with it, entire patches of arcane detail you thought you'd forgotten: the names of your undergraduate professors; that weird Christian Science kid you kissed as a high school freshman, and regretted; the exact layout of your brothers' tree fort; where you hid your precious beach finds, shells and sea glass, as a child. And younger still, you remember the bird, drunk on firethorn berries, that dove into your bedroom window over and over again until it killed itself. You recall the patch of scarlet feathers under its wings when you poked it with a stick and mourned its suicide.

Time is broken into these compartments. The distant past. The endless present. And the only future is your release date. Everyone keeps a calendar. They draw the months out and cross off the days. Eventually, I succumb, too. The first thing anyone asks you is "How much time do you have?" As if time is currency, which I will learn in some ways it is. If you are fighting a case—say, a murder charge—you will be in jail for years before you are finally sentenced to prison, because in spite of what everyone thinks, there are no speedy trials. Not for the poor. Not for people of color. Which means not for their victims, either. The victims of your crime will live, sometimes for years, in a state of suspense and disbelief. And because of such relatively long, hard time in county jail, you are given perks. You get to sleep in the Dayroom, where three-tiered bunks are lined up against the walls because overcrowding means there aren't enough cells for housing prisoners. Dayroom gives you access to movement. To *less* incarceration. More time, ironically, equals more freedom, so the more violent your crime, the better off your circumstances of incarceration.

More time means you can be a "trustee." This means you work, and work passes time. You serve the food and delegate toilet cleaning to your fellow prisoners. You get first stab at the clean blues, blankets, underwear, sheets, and socks that come once a week. You are first for commissary. You aren't locked up all day, and you watch over your fellow prisoners. You are in with the deputies. For this reason, I call them "kapos," the name given to the Jewish prisoners in the Holocaust who received moderately better treatment than their doomed fellow Jews because they worked for the Nazis. For instance, they threw the dead bodies of their neighbors, brothers, and sisters into the incinerators after they were gassed. For all their treachery to their own people, most of the kapos were killed in the end anyway.

Every week, a box from Amazon arrives. Every day, the letters. They perforate the monotony, the dullness that seeps into everything. If I get one letter, I save it, maybe for after lunch. If two or more letters arrive in one day, I spread them out on my metal slab and gaze at them. They are priceless. My record in one day was seven letters. I remember that number because in jail you count and count and count. I reread every letter several times. Almost always, the first sentence of every letter is: "I cannot begin to imagine what it feels like . . ."

One of the people who wrote to me every single day was a writing student of mine named Vicki. In fact, all my students from the same writing class wrote to me. I'd begun teaching the class a few weeks before I'd found out that I was going to be prosecuted and sent to jail.

After about the tenth letter from Vicki, I took a moment to fully comprehend her gift to me, and the gift of that class, and how it came to be that my students, all upstanding Jewish citizens, wrote to their jailed writing teacher with such fierce loyalty. Some even sent me their stories to edit and I was grateful for the chance to occupy myself with work I loved to do.

It happened this way: I was a couple months sober and had no idea I would be prosecuted the way I was, when out of the blue I received a call from Lisa Rosenbaum, a writer who I'd once worked with in a critique group. She was now working at the Jewish Women's Theatre at The Braid, a nonprofit theater in Santa Monica. In addition to the theater events they sponsored and created, Ronda, The Braid's artistic director and cofounder, wanted to launch creative writing classes. They needed a teacher. Would I do it?

I jumped at the chance and said I would. I was sober, my family was slowly repairing, and I was cleaning up my life, one tiny bit at a time. I had not yet even been to court, but I spoke to my attorney and he assured me I would not do jail time. I would probably get a lot of community service, he said, a year of DUI classes, and maybe drug testing. So I took the job.

The first day of class went a thousand miles to improving my self-esteem. The students were all women, most of whom were older than me, but like me, Jewish in a mainly secular way. They were glorious, beautiful women, familiar to me, people I *knew* in my heart. I remember Greg had to drive me across town every class because my license had been revoked, and he met Vicki. He said, "She's a saucy one." He loved her. And all the others, mostly because he saw how happy they made me, and how wonderful I felt teaching again, when none of my former employers, like UCLA, would give me another chance. They were women from the tribe, with mannerisms and language smattered with Yiddish, and a Jewish worldview that was familiar and comfortable to me.

The Braid felt like home.

When I was sentenced to jail, to my surprise and heartbreak, I knew I would have to tell both Lisa and Ronda. I didn't know what that would mean for the class, though my attorney assured me repeatedly I'd be out in four days. There was no reason anymore to believe a word out of his mouth—by then I couldn't stand the guy for all his bullshit—but hope does strange things to one's grasp on reality. If that were true, I reasoned, I'd miss only one day.

I called and spoke first to Lisa, who was surprised by the news, but entirely calm and understanding; the kind of response you'd like from someone during an earthquake or a bank robbery. I said I wanted to tell my students in person; they deserved that much. But when Ronda heard she was, understandably, very unhappy, and thinking at first that I had taken the job knowing I'd have to go to jail, she had different idea for the way things would go. I was to write a letter to my students and she would attach a postscript. Eventually Ronda, who in every respect is a visionary artist and compassionate woman, came to see that I had not lied. At first, though, things were tense, and of course, I didn't blame her for being upset. I did as she asked and wrote a long letter to my dear students. I left nothing out. It was one of the hardest things I ever had to do.

Ronda attached a note in the email, with an apology on behalf of The Braid. She provided the students with three choices. First, they could continue the class, with a break till I was released. Second, we could do the remaining two sessions before I left and receive a refund for the remainder, or third, we'd end now, and they would get 80 percent of their money back. The Braid would proceed based on the decision of the group. She gave them a day to decide.

It is impossible to describe what it felt like reading that email when it appeared in my in-box. I remember lying on the couch in my office afterward, crestfallen and sick with self-hatred. My friend Anadel was there, as always, and I remember telling her how bad I felt for once again screwing up other people's lives. Even in sobriety, it seemed like I was doing everything wrong.

Then my email pinged. Then it pinged again. And again, and again. Ten times. One after the other. I got up to look, and to my amazement, every single one of my students had responded within minutes of receiving the letter. Almost all at the same time, in one giant reply-all email.

I read the first email that I could see, but it was really the fifth in a series.

Dear Lisa and Leslie,

We bonded the first night we met. Leslie spoke of being honest, digging deep, having the courage to tell our stories. You have done just that, Leslie, with this beautiful note you've written. I would also vote for continuing the class and pausing for whatever period of time required. I feel you, Leslie, fit my ideal of a writing teacher and I don't want to let go of this opportunity to work with you! And I want to quickly add that I already feel we, as a class, have established a level of trust and compassion and determination that is rare. So onward ho with the writing class!

We will be with you, Leslie, as you go through this passage in your life.

I look forward to seeing everyone again— tomorrow evening?

All Best Wishes,
Cely

"Anadel," I said. "Look."

She leaned over and looked at the long thread of emails, pages and pages of letters from my students expressing their love, their allegiance, their devotion, their acceptance, their desire to continue and wait for me no matter how long I would be locked up.

Anadel and I looked at each other, and then at the same time, we both fell apart, holding each other and crying. I realized at that moment that my students had invited me back to my Jewishness. Not back to teaching, not back to work, but back to God.

In lockup, when I receive letters, I always break from reading my books to write back to everyone who has written. I am forced, like a five-year-old, to write with an itty-bitty golf pencil on brown recycled paper, all purchased for 50 percent more than their value from commissary

Every day, I write a letter to my husband.

> *I want you to know how much I love you. I miss you*
> *so much . . . it feels like the privations and the scarcity*
> *in this place sometimes open something up, an*
> *expansiveness, like I'm looking down on all the*
> *goodness in you, every beautiful aspect of you, a kind*
> *of surprise and awe . . .*

Or:

> *Fuck this place. I fucking hate this place. What*
> *fucked-up God would put the idea of jail in the hearts*
> *of men? Especially for the many in here who are*
> *nonviolent, who need help, not incarceration.*

Or:

We've been mercilessly yelled at, punished, locked
down, called bitches, humiliated by that deputy . . .
How I detest her. If anything jail has taught me how
to hate.

I write every detail of my experience. I lament the way society has thrown so many people away. I note with horror that most of them are black and brown. I make sure every detail of the abuse by deputies is listed. And I ask Greg to keep the letters. I want them as a witness to the depravity of power, but also as a narrative of my endurance.

When the books arrive, it's better than anything I have ever known. Better than sex. Better than drugs or alcohol. Better than recovery. Better than daytime. Better than the moon. It is better than free samples at the mall. Better than the sound of an owl when morning is barely an idea and the stars still carpet the sky. When I open these books, I imagine my entire cell filling up with the words inside. The books are brand-new so I take a deep whiff of the paper and glue. I bury my nose in the spine.

I know that I have a lot of time on my hands. One jail day is the equivalent to three really shitty normal life days. So when I start a book, I read every word very slowly. It is the first time I feel cursed by my ability to read fast, though perhaps not thoroughly. The books will teach me, then, how to slow down. I feel the sentences stretch along the space-time continuum. Each word fills my mouth. A vowel is confection: flan or frosting. Consonants are piquant and crunchy: sauerkraut. Sometimes the words crawl up my spine.

Other times, I see the words encircling the toilet, the sink, the piece of warped steel they call a mirror. One by one, the words march off the page and get cozy with my bunkie. They block out the noise, the constant sound of toilets flushing, the incessant crinkle of plastic unfurling from the commissary candy, the click of the locks, the doors slamming, the deputies shrieking. Their never-ending insults. And the sad, overmuch laughter of the inmates penetrating through the cinder block walls.

I have time to think about these things. To think about the way a book feels in my hand, or tastes, or sounds. I have never loved so hard and with such fidelity and reciprocation. Books can break your heart, but they never leave you.

I read Mary Oliver in desultory, languid fashion, the way I might if I were home in bed and it were raining outside. I imagine it: I am pleasantly bored. I pick the book up from the stack on the floor by my bed. I flip through it, and then it happens; I am lifted up out of malaise and find inspiration in the loveliness of gray cleansing skies, the comfort of home, and the words that seem to fall out of the pages like snow.

I pretend I am there, but this is hard and it doesn't last long. To think of home is a magician's trick that I haven't quite mastered. One day, while Duckie is downstairs in class, I pick the book of Oliver's poems up and off my stack. I am aware that I am just putting off the inevitable, which is finishing this one and cracking open the next book that lies in its stack of three beneath my bunk. I am hung up on reducing the stack to one down, two to go. I am so afraid of finishing all the books before the next ones arrive that I agonize over the disturbance of my stack each time I absent one from it. But I know, too, with some solace, that poetry is never finished. Should I run out of books, I tell myself, as I listen to the blue-clad students downstairs shouting out answers to remedial math problems, I can always return to a poem and *always* find something new about it.

The one I fall into now is called "One or Two Things." Oliver begins with a command to be left alone because her birth has just occurred. The three lines of this edict in the opening stanza of the poem are simple and bold; being born is private and arduous, so go away.

It would have been impossible at that moment in medical to see the comma that Melissa and I made of our bodies as my birth. I could not have seen that first cell as my womb. In the darkness of betrayal, you cannot see beyond the feeling that the world has abandoned you, that you have abandoned yourself as surely as you have deserted those you love. It is too tricky to contemplate this when the sore is festering and you live in the wounds. But maybe that moment, its sacredness was the sacredness of birth.

The poem continues on for seven stanzas that she enumerates

as chapters. My favorites fall toward the end. In the poem, Oliver professes that we require very little for survival, much less for happiness. Eternity doesn't exist, so stop thinking you're never going to die. It is a poem that points its finger at me. Don't be greedy; use only what you need. I am reminded as I read it that without adversity and misfortune I would not know abundance. When Oliver steps into the poem, and invites us into her truth—that she labored to love and cherish her life—I feel myself gaining strength. An infinitesimally small light wavers in the dark.

I enjoy a lingering thought—it repeats itself in my mind: *Poetry is alive.* But sometimes in the moment, when you read it, a poem makes no sense. You don't recognize yourself in it. The words are suspended in ridiculousness and disbelief. This is what faith is: waiting to believe. Maybe poetry is simply there to comfort and anoint, rather than explain and define our lives. With poetry, you may find yourself in it more fully, more completely the second, third, tenth time you read. You will understand now what you didn't understand then. As I read Oliver I come to see that poetry is like evolution. It changes with new conditions; it is something that continuously branches into new directions and diversifies in meaning. It has arms that will wrap themselves around you when you are in need of such love. But as with all true love, a poem will also let you rest in its language without forcing meaning on you until you are ready for it.

Mary Oliver shows me the things that matter: love and our essential connection to the natural world. Her poems make it clear that our gods and our gurus aren't human, that, in fact, maybe they shouldn't be. "One or Two Things" is a warning poem. Don't try so hard to love your life because, like the butterfly that lifts off on such light and insubstantial wings, all life is ephemeral, all life vanishes.

I can learn from the butterfly about my ego and my grasping attachments to my life in a far more profound way than I can ever learn from another human being, or from the brick and mortar of religion. That she chooses a butterfly, not the caterpillar, not the chrysalis, tells me as I read it in lockup that metamorphosis does not come without suffering, patience, and wisdom. The caterpillar/chrysalis trope might be cliché, especially in midlife. But I am grateful for the reminder the poem provides. And with that gratitude comes a startling thought: I have wasted a lot of time being a literary snob. It occurs to me that I don't have to be the cynic I normally am and say things like, "Mary Oliver is a little too popular for my tastes." I realize that my intellectualism has made my world small. That even in reading, my ego has diminished possibility. I feel like I've stumbled on a secret.

When I read the poems that evoke the outdoors—most of Oliver's poems do—I am pained beyond belief. In my real life, I am a camper, a hiker. I have slept under the moon, swum with sea turtles the size of my dining room table. I once backpacked in the Denali Wilderness and slumbered in a tent while grizzlies roamed through the brush nearby. One winter, I hiked Arches in Utah, in the snow, at dusk, and watched the stars pop into the sky one by one, like a Van Gogh painting.

That I cannot go outside now makes the reality a formidable one. There are no trees to put pencils in. There are no stars, there is no moon. Ever. The air we breathe is fetid with bodies and rage. I long for the butterfly that has already been freed of its cocoon, for the scent of rainy woods, salty oceans, the delicious sting of fresh, cold snow. I remember one morning before jail, when my daughter found a nattily striped caterpillar in our garden inching along the milkweed I'd planted. I hear her voice now in my cell. "Whoa, Mom. Look!" Few things impress my adolescent daughter, and I was happy for a moment in that long, anxiety-fueled buildup to jail that she saw the beauty in that critter. We looked it up to try to identify it, our heads touching as we angled for position over the Google search on her phone. We were charmed to see that the caterpillar would one day morph into a monarch. I remember promising to take her to Natural Bridges State Beach in the winter, where the monarchs gather during their migration. I say to her, "Each monarch weighs less than a gram, but they migrate eighteen hundred miles round-trip *every year*."

Whoa, Mom.

The joy of this memory is destroyed when Duckie returns and I hear the deputy shout, "Hurry up and shut the door, Rodriguez." It slams. The lock clicks. I revisit this idea, that I do not get to see the sky for weeks. What I will see daily is a locked steel door. And Melissa on that grim, bleak night in medical. It felt like years ago that she lay down beside me. I remember then that I did not feel powerful. I felt depleted, annihilated. Destroyed. I did not see evolution or renewal, not then. I wonder; when the baby bursts into the world from that oceanic safety of the womb, does she feel similarly disempowered? Is not our life the constant struggle for authenticity, for compassion, for love? Who says we are only born once? Or that birth is anything but the desire for transformation?

CHAPTER THREE

Pregnant Module

Everything in the universe is constantly changing, and nothing stays the same, and we must understand how quickly time flows by if we are to wake up and truly live our lives. That's what it means to be a time being.
—Ruth Ozeki, *A Tale for the Time Being*

After I have read all of Oliver, I must move forward. I am not even two full weeks in, and, like every other thing in jail, the date when my next three books will arrive remains unknown. Inmates live in a constant state of unknowing. It is one of their tricks—keeping us guessing, always on edge. I am told I am in permanent housing now. So I comfort myself: *Your books will arrive regularly now that you aren't wandering anymore in that no-man's-land of receiving.* I attempt to convince myself that there is stability.

I put Oliver down and I pick up *A Tale for the Time Being.* As I have done with every book since my childhood, I examine the cover. I read every single word on it. I look at the cover image, the jacket design. The author photo and bio. After I published my first novel, I began also looking at the acknowledgments to see who'd been thanked. There was a time when my name began to appear in the acknowledgments of other writers' books, a small thrill to see.

I had no idea what Ozeki's book was about, only that it had received rave reviews when it came out—something about a lunchbox washing up onshore in Canada after the tsunami in Japan. So imagine my surprise when I read the first page: "A time being is someone who lives in time, and that means you, and me, and every one of us who is, or was, or ever will be."

Did Ruth Ozeki know me? Was she writing to me? Did she know I was living in suspended time, real time, unreal time? *Did she know I was in jail?* Of course not, and yet . . .

A Tale for the Time Being is many stories in one book. It is about Japanese manga culture, it is about Buddhism, it is about global warming, the Japanese earthquake, and the subsequent horror of the tsunami and the nuclear meltdown. Sometimes it is about bullying. Also, culture and identity. Female empowerment. If you want to, you could say it is about island manners or human encroachment on the environment. It could be simply about barnacles and black crows, if that is where your mind is headed. And no one would mistake its passionate antiwar theme.

But, for me, this book was about love and loss, and a friendship transacted through time. Floating to my lips as I read, the narrative of love and isolation, loneliness and connection, gave me my breath. I saw that I was being given instructions about how to work with pain. Impermanence, change, time: these were the concepts I grasped for and held onto from Ozeki's work.

The story begins when a Hello Kitty lunchbox washes ashore on a remote Canadian island. One of the main characters, Ruth, finds the lunchbox and discovers within it a journal hidden inside the cover of Proust's *À la recherche du temps perdu*, letters, and a wristwatch. Ruth believes, as she reads the tragic journal of sixteen-year-old Nao, that it has washed ashore after the tsunami.

In alternating points of view, we learn about Nao's highly pressurized life in Tokyo, of her father's failure to provide for his family and his subsequent suicide attempts, of the violent bullying Nao sustains at school (and even the bullying she passes on to another), and about her great-grandmother, Jiko, a Buddhist nun who changes her life.

Ruth is living on an island in Canada with her husband, an eccentric brilliant environmentalist and artist. Her mother has just died after her battle with Alzheimer's, and Ruth, a New York City transplant, is becoming increasingly critical of small-town life as she falls deeper and deeper into Nao's narrative. Ruth, a writer, is also stuck in time—with writer's block. She writes:

> *Time interacts with attention in funny ways. At one extreme, when Ruth was gripped by the compulsive mania and hyperfocus of an Internet search, the hours seemed to*

aggregate and swell like a wave, swallowing huge chunks
of her day. At the other extreme, when her attention was
disengaged and fractured, she experienced time at its
most granular, wherein moments hung around like par-
ticles, diffused and suspended in standing water.

When I read that, I put the book down. I looked out the teeny-tiny window of my cell into the module at the stopped clock and laughed. How true: granular, diffused, suspended, not for me in water, but cement. I am struck also, while reading the alternating points of view, by the circuitous nature of narrative, how story is never linear. This is true for my own life, where 414 days are interrupted by a glitch in the chronology, a world newly inhabited by ghosts and demons. I suspect grief does this, too, but also joy, our contemporary lives interrupted and changed by circumstances; in my case, seemingly halted by what I don't remember.

Where did that time go? If I don't remember it, does that mean it doesn't exist? And how could I locate myself in a narrative that did not exist in my memory? After I began to recover, I decided to find out what I had done during that time, who I had hurt, and how. I literally had no idea. I spent nearly two years collecting the information of those 414 days; information that came in the form of police reports, ER medical records, rehab notes, and even interviews that I conducted with the dozens of people who attempted to save my life during that time (including my husband, my best friend Anadel, my daughter, the paramedics who revived me after overdoses, doctors, cops, and neighbors). The documents, thirteen pounds of them, take up an entire drawer of a large filing cabinet. That patchwork of information, and the stories other people told me, helped me re-create a story in my mind of what had happened and how, drunk and hooked on drugs, I had managed to fall into such a state of mental illness that I did the terrible things I did.

But it isn't really *my* story. It is their story of my story.

"You weren't here for any of it," Greg said. "We were the ones who had to live through it."

And given the trauma they experienced, clearly their version of events is tinged with anger and sadness. I can never reclaim those lost chapters of my life. To understand what I did, so that I could make real amends to the people I hurt, was both a devastating and a life-altering experience. I have no regrets about taking such drastic measures in order to uncover at least some version of what happened during that relapse, even if that version was someone else's of what transpired. But, as Ozeki's book shows me, memory and experience are skewered by time. The experience of my life here is not the same as the way it would have been lived out there.

As I read, amid my loneliness and my disbelief—how could *this* be my life?—I worried that I would never make sense of myself, of the time I had lost, of the past recovery that I had thrown away, of the future that appeared bleak, inscrutable, and impossible to imagine. It seemed to me that like Nao, who could not comprehend the cruelty and unfairness of her circumstances, I was wide-awake in a world I could never have imagined.

When the subject of bullying arose in Nao's life, I couldn't put the book down. My fellow inmates and I were constantly bullied, name-called, and in some cases physically abused by our captors, the youngest and most inexperienced members of the LA County Sheriff's Department. These were ambitious people striving for position in the department, wishing to do anything but jail time themselves. Which just made it worse for us.

At school, Nao is bullied by her classmates. They call her the "transfer student." Essentially raised in America, she doesn't conform to Japanese custom, she doesn't *feel* innately, culturally Japanese. And her otherness, painful, ironic (it makes no sense to her, confuses her; she is, after all, of Japanese parentage), eggs on her classmates, even her teacher. But in Japan, when a man can't provide for his family, the entire family is shamed. Nao is poor. She lives in a one-room apartment in Tokyo. Her bullies are merciless. She is taunted and physically tortured. The others pinch and burn and hit her. She is covered in bruises. The cruelty, as detailed by Ozeki, was piercing to read, unflinchingly written and scary. I loved Ozeki for her refusal to write small.

The bullying by the deputies—inmates called them "po-lice"—was unfathomable. We were called "bitches," "idiots," "stupid," and once we were called "insects." I watched guards drag women from their cells for unknown reasons and bring them to the

Dayroom, where everyone could see them strip-searched, patted down, handcuffed, and then thrown out into the recreation area and chained to chairs. One day, a young woman was escorted by two stone-faced deputies back from somewhere, beaten to a pulp. She hadn't looked like that in the morning when they'd taken her away.

"That's the elevator ride beatdown," Duckie told me.

"Elevator ride?"

"They go for a ride in the elevator looking good; they come back later bloody."

The outside world rarely hears about such abuses. And from my experience, most people don't believe it happens. Yet, in 2016, the FBI's probe into jailhouse abuse in LA County's men's central jail (they said they were probing the women's jail, too, but that was just another lie) ended in the conviction of six deputies and two superiors, including LA County Sherriff's top cop, Lee Baca. Each time another one of them was hauled away in handcuffs, I admit, I celebrated. Compared to mentally ill addicts and their petty crimes, the abuse of power and the violence by people wearing uniforms nauseated me.

While I saw what went on between deputies and inmates, it became clear it was not the inmates I needed to fear, but our guards. And I can't say I was afraid they would hurt me—I was white, first of all, and had the resources to make trouble for them. I was more afraid of my response to them. They were not, as a rule, very bright, and it seemed to me when dumb people had the tacit approval to hurt others, the abuse was coarse and visible. They didn't need to employ stealthy tactics: mob mentality, implicitly approved by the overseeing power, never has to hide its violence.

My biggest fear was that I would lose self-control. I worried that I would retaliate for their brutality and say what I thought about them to their faces as I had when I was arrested. To keep silent was one of the most labored experiences in my life. Anywhere else, I would have said something. But I had already made the mistake of calling police Nazi motherfuckers, and for that, being charged with battery. Though the arrest report, a defamatory mess of additions and deletions, rewritten and revised over several days, makes claims in an addendum that I bit an officer, there is no evidence that I bit or "battered" an officer. The truth, that I never touched him, matters not at all. It's a waste of breath to attempt a defense. Drunk versus cop. Who do you think wins?

Nao, too, never flinched. She never fought back, either. She took it. Like we did. This is the advantage that bullies enjoy. Unmediated power. When not held accountable, that knife is a sharp and effective one to wield.

Nao's difference made her invisible. Her voice had been taken by bullies and the parents who did not understand her. I remember when I read this how I had to put the book down to catch my breath. The anguish I experienced was acute, not just for my own sense of having been forgotten, of not being *seen*, but for everyone in lockup. Outside my cell lived the largely black and Latina population, the mentally ill, the addicted, the raped, the sexually abused, the uneducated, the poor, the beaten. Women whose silence is so deep, so profound, they shout, they break laws, they kill themselves, hoping someone will listen, and still, they are greeted by nothing. Disempowered. Invisibility is an epidemic in jail, as it is also the thing that lies beneath addiction, poverty, social exclusion, and being female.

Nao turns to her great-grandmother, the wise old Jiko, for help understanding her pain. It confuses her because, as I, too, learn, all good wisdom is hard to understand at first. Trying to make sense of the words old Jiko uses to characterize her experience, Nao writes in her journal: "I think it means that nothing in the world is solid or real, because nothing is permanent, and all things—including trees and animals and pebbles and mountains and rivers and even me and you—are just kind of flowing through for the time being."

At Lynwood, then, I was flowing through for the time being. I was forced to face impermanence. Impermanence is a nice idea, but lockup seemed endless and abusive, like something I wore that was always too tight around the throat and belly. Ephemerality might be true, but you still have to live in your pain until it ends.

One day, Duckie asked, "Were you afraid when you saw me?"

"No," I answered truthfully.

"Huh," she said.

It was always difficult to understand Duckie, because she'd lost almost all her teeth to crystal meth. She was sentenced to a year for possession of six pounds of marijuana with intent to sell. Usually county jail took only misdemeanors and nonviolent crimes, but because the prisons, which house felons, were overcrowded, the legislature in California enacted a bill called AB 109. This made it possible for county jail to house nonviolent felons, slated for state prison, whose sentences were a year or less. Trading Band-Aid fixes for wisdom, the legislation perpetuated the overcrowding issue in California rather than addressing it. Because she was sentenced to a year, she had six months to serve on AB 109. She would be out a month after me, having served most of her time when I met her.

"My husband beat me and took my children," Duckie said one day, weeping. She wept all the time. And when Duckie didn't weep, she sang Mexican ballads in Spanish. She had a beautiful voice. She also ate hard-boiled eggs and pickles and the foulest of commissary foods she could get without fail in the jail cell. I hid my gagging in my bedding. At night, she snored like a sea lion. Never before or after have I heard anything like it—it was Olympic-class snoring, gold medal worthy.

"The first thing I'm going to do when I get out is get my teeth," she said. "Praise Jesus."

She said that she was locked up in the highest security unit of the jail, brought in on a 5150 psych hold from under the bridge downtown where she was living.

"Then God took pity on me and moved me here. To Pregnant Dorm."

It was in Pregnant Dorm that she converted to Christianity and found Jesus. She repented breaking the law, including the prostitution she engaged in to pay for her habit. She had big plans for her release. In addition to getting her teeth fixed, she'd find housing, vocational training, a job. She'd been on the streets for so long, she didn't know how to do much of anything. Abused, addicted, beaten by her husband, cast out by family, prostitution, selling drugs, doing time, losing time, spending time, avoiding time. That was her life.

"I love my babies," she said, speaking of her adult children. Weeping. "He took them from me. Kicked me out the door. I am so ashamed. I was nothing after that, nothing."

There was one section of Ozeki's book that changed my life so profoundly that, as I read it, I felt a physical shift sweep through my body. I have never experienced anything like it before, where quite literally I knew after having read it that I was a different person. It was like watching my old ideas fall from a bridge and splash into the water below.

It began with a section about the shame Nao's dad felt after designing an interface for the gaming market that prompted the US military to inquire about using it for real warfare. Nao's dad wanted to install a "conscience" into the software so it couldn't be used for mass destruction. He recognizes his desire to change the interface as a good act, but one motivated by a weak impulse—shame. It was the very same sensibility that lurked behind his decision to put such destruction into the universe in the first place.

Nao's dad explains how the "politicians" in Japan have tried changing history by erasing the horrors of Manchu from the history books to ease the "culture of shame" in which the Japanese exist. "By changing our history and our memory, they try to erase all our shame. This is why I think shame must be different from conscience. . . . Shame comes from the outside, but conscience must be a natural feeling that comes from a deep place inside an individual person."

All of a sudden, sitting there in my cell, I comprehended what a stealthy foe shame is. All it really wanted was for me to die in a pool of self-pity. I saw with amazing clarity its ridiculousness as I realized how shame as a state of mind so readily stood in the way of a person's ability to redeem their bad behavior.

On the inside cover of Ozeki's book, I wrote a list of how I thought shame destroyed people. It read as follows:

1. Keeps us mired in the belief that we *are* the sum total of our deeds. We mope around in the past.
2. While living in it, we slip out of the reality of our present.
3. It's not real. It comes from the outside. Like a prosecutor, keeping you in line, by impugning your spirit. Un-divine.

4. Shame blinds us to our goodness. And when the good in us is in the shadows of self-hatred, we are incapable of acknowledging or fixing our wrongs.

5. Shame wants us dead. It's the impetus behind every suicide. Therefore it serves no evolutionary function. If shame is useless, then I can let it go.

Writing this, I realized that when in shame, we stuff our potential for reconciliation into the darkness of our disgrace. It's different from guilt, because in shame, we believe we *are* bad, while in guilt we believe we *did* bad. But what Ozeki tells us is that conscience is where transcendence really lies. It was the thing Nao's dad was after, that deep, whole place within that knows right from wrong, that teaches us to act—in the Buddhist sense—lawfully.

I put the book down and tallied my estimable acts, all the things I had done long before all of this jail nonsense. No one, not a single person, and certainly not a prosecutor or a jailer, had to tell me that I needed to make financial and personal amends. My conscience was my only voice. I tracked down the guy whose car I smashed while parking drunk and wrote him a check for repairs the week I returned from rehab. I gave him the money and told him I was sorry. I began the long hard work of family therapy, at first dragging my family into something that made them afraid. Later they began to appreciate the opportunity to talk about how much I'd hurt them, without fear of reprisal—they were third-party safe. And while that was in motion, I made a list of all my harms and began to seek out the people who deserved my amends. I even contacted LAPD. Two of the many officers I encountered were gracious, utterly forgiving, and to this day, they each check up on me, sending me emails, congratulating me every year I stay sober, wishing me well. The good of that helped mitigate the horror of my last arrest, and the arresting officers' cowardly assault on me.

I remember it was night when I read that passage, and the jail was restless as usual. I placed Ozeki's book under my bunk. I stood up and, while Duckie snored, looked out the tiny window. Rain was falling heavily and had made Christmas lights out of the flood lamps on the side of the building. It looked like jewels were falling to the ground, and for a moment the scene seemed so beautiful and tender. I knew that I had crossed some kind of long bridge to self-worth and merit. I said these words to myself: *You are an amazing person. You are a good citizen. You are a loving wife and mother. You are a loyal friend.*

No jail sentence could ever eclipse the goodness inside my heart, that place in the darkness that Ozeki's book shined a light on.

∞

For all her sorrow, Duckie cracked me up. She was so funny. Completely out of control, it seemed, of her physical body. I remember once, while she was showering, I heard her let out a hair-raising scream. She ran back toward our cell shrieking, clutching a skimpy, jail-issued towel around her flubbery, ample body. Her hair, already unruly, was practically electrified by terror, and she couldn't seem to gain speed with her weight and fumbling feet clad in plastic shower shoes.

"There's worms in the shower," she bellowed. "You can't do that shit to me, man. I'm schizophrenic."

Even though I knew she was scared, I could not stop laughing. And there *were* worms, not worm hallucinations. They were small and undulating in large numbers at the drain. Later the janitors or jailers, I was not sure which, came in and sprayed the showers, and at Duckie's insistence, the drain to our cell sink. The poison was so toxic that she came back from class to find me literally passed out from the fumes and dragged me out of the cell, screaming hysterically to the deputy on duty, a small man who seemed frightened of her, "You've just killed a writer. That's not gonna look good for you, man."

Duckie was huge, and she ate unceasingly. But she was also modest. She would never take a shit if I was in the cell. I knew to give her that privacy during program. She also never showed her private parts when she changed her clothing. I knew it made her uncomfortable so I would suddenly have to read or look at a letter when she changed.

She also loved school and was so proud of her grades. Every A she received in the jail's school, she made sure to show me.

And, no surprise, she was also a hustler. She basically ran Pregnant Dorm.

While she was in school, other inmates—trustees—would come by.

Miss Jones: "Hello, Leslie. Good morning. May you be blessed today."

One day, while Duckie was in school, Juana, a Duckie friend and trustee, came by. "Vanessa says you wanted to go to Catholic services, so we'll pop your door when they start."

I couldn't remember telling her I wanted to go to Catholic services. I'm a Jew. But there were no services for Jews, and though I'd heard tell of a female rabbi—a notorious bitch who rubbed your face in your misdeeds—I'd never seen her. Once, reportedly, she took away an inmate's medically ordered kosher meal because she wasn't a Jew, she was African American. I requested to see her anyway, but she never showed up, which was probably a blessing. As a Jew, I felt completely alone inside.

But it was clear that Duckie, whose kindness and sensitivity was louder than her crass exterior, knew being locked up twenty-three hours a day was killing me, so she arranged for me to get out for all the Christian services, an hour every time outside my cell. Though I hated church, I was grateful to Duckie for making sure I could get out and move around. Going to church was a habit I repeated in every module, because it got me out of that cell. Still, listening to Jesus this and damnation that was excruciating—and I would spend that hour contemplating which was worse: lockup or church. Toss up.

Duckie also managed to procure virgin underwear for me, six pairs, size small, which I kept the entire time, washing them in the sink. For the duration of my sentence, I never had to wear underwear that had been visited by countless vaginas before mine. She also found thermals for me *in my size*. There were so few small sizes that nothing fit me. I never wore anything but XXL blues and I tripped over them incessantly. The few sets of blues, bras, socks, and thermals they had in smaller sizes were always taken by the kapos and sold to the chosen for commissary.

One day, after complaining about the unending sciatic nerve pain that I was afflicted with, Duckie stood up and went to the door. She was always screaming out orders in Spanish to the other inmates through the door.

She called out for one of the kapos, who came to our cell, took a note, and kited it (which means carried it, against rules, to another cell) to the door of an inmate in a cell across from our tier. In a few minutes, she returned with a handful of ibuprofens that she slipped under the door.

"Here you go," Duckie said casually, handing them over. All in a day's work. No big deal.

I was astonished, and grateful. "Thanks," I said.

"Don't mention it."

She never asked for trade in kind. When my money came, I told Duckie to order whatever she wanted on my account. I entrusted her with my log-on. She could have taken advantage of me, but she didn't. She only ordered envelopes, coffee, a Styrofoam cup, and fireball candy (for her coffee). Honor in jail existed. All of my bunkies observed a code of respect and honesty.

During program, while I wandered aimlessly, unsure what to do, who to talk to, when to shower, Duckie would stand off to the side and watch people, making sure no one bothered me. Imprisonment had been her way of life. She knew the inside of lockup the way I knew the subtleties of a teaching syllabus. If anyone even remotely looked at me crosswise, she intervened.

"You have a problem," she said to me one day, "you just call Duckie, and I'll take care of it."

I cannot fathom why Duckie took me under her wing. Later, I saw a pattern in jail, of being utterly and completely cared for. It happened over and over again—the people I encountered showing me only love, kindness, and respect—as long as they were inmates.

Often Duckie and I sat together during the countless, endless hours, biding time. Passing time, wasting time, killing time, squandering time. And yet I felt so present, so real, so painfully alive, that I could not imagine, like Nao could, that my physical body or my place in Lynwood was impermanent. I quickly learned that jail incarcerates time as well. But it incarcerates everything. I remember once, staring out my tiny window, alone in my cell, I saw a bird fluttering in the rafters. How it got there,

I don't know, but it was something I saw in every module I was moved to, and it always shocked me.

About eight days into my stay in Pregnant Dorm, the deputy called me. This one loved to use the loudspeaker, which meant you could never understand a word she said. It was just noise bouncing off the walls. So at first, I had no idea I was being called. Duckie says, "Go down there. They're calling you."

"You've got a visitor," the deputy says. It's my husband. I don't want to go. I don't want anyone ever to see me like this. I am too depressed to talk to anyone about anything. But I know that if I decline the visit Greg will be crushed. The visiting room is just outside the module, a cold narrow place with eight seats on two sides of the double-pained bulletproof plexiglass. I am set free—unaccompanied, that is—for one minute as I walk between the door of the module and the door of the visiting room. Ten steps of freedom. Except, of course, for the cameras and the guard in her bulletproof cube watching me.

There he is. His smile kills me. Greg is singularly handsome, his face an angel face. Strangers on the street think he's a movie star. One thing my daughter always tells me—the two of them butt heads because they are so similar, so I am my daughter's confidant—is how much she loves the ever-present smile on his face.

When things went bad during my relapse, Greg took our daughter out of the house. I was too wasted at the time to know where they went. I remember that I could not sleep anymore. I lay in the darkness, alone in the bed Greg and I once shared, waiting for light so I could replenish my well. It seemed that no matter how hard I tried to leave enough vodka for the morning to stave off the DTs and the wasteland of my life, I often failed, and would rise in darkness and wait through the hours until 6 a.m. when I could buy a drink, usually in the form of a bottle from Vons, CVS, or Ralphs. These hours were the worst kind of loneliness and I often thought how much better it might be to die. Once I drank again, the memory of my family's goneness was obliterated.

When I got clean, Greg said, "Make no mistake; if you ever touch a substance again, I will be gone so fast you won't see me leaving."

It was probably the best thing anyone ever said to me. He meant it. Such words might sound harsh, but sometimes the only thing you can do to help a drunk is leave them lying in the gutter in order to save your own life. Ironically, doing so often saves the addict's life as well.

Now he looks sad and joyful all at once behind the plastic bulletproof barrier, the imprint of kissing lips and hands from those on both sides trying to make a connection creating shadows on his skin.

His face is filled with love. It shatters me.

"Hey," I say.

"Hey."

I have nothing to say, so I spew my rage. Instead of sparing my beloved any more agony than he is already going through, I tell him I wish I were dead. I tell him how bad it is. I rage and rage. He sits there, helpless. I am unable to ask him about our daughter or the dog or my friends because to mention what I yearn for is like a fire in my throat. The only way I can do my isolation is to stay that way, allow nothing from out there in here.

We have thirty agonizing minutes together. When the visit ends I tell him not to come back. The visit is a source of such extreme pain that it takes me the rest of the day and most of the next day to stop the thrumming sorrow in my body.

"Please," I tell him on the phone. "Don't come."

I don't want him to see what I have become. But he comes back, repeatedly, and offers what love he can behind the glass. When I ask him once why he stayed with me through the relapse, he says, "Because when I married you I took a vow to honor you in sickness and in health."

At my request, he never brings our daughter. I make arrangements to have no other visitors, though there is a list at home of twenty or more friends who *want* to come.

"No," I say, the one time I call Anadel. "This is no place for anyone."

I don't call anyone except Greg and our daughter, and once, my friend Kim; only two times did I call Anadel, the one person, besides my husband, who did not even consider leaving me alone as I struggled with early sobriety and the prospect of jail. But I don't want to see them. I have nothing to say. Jail steals time. It also stole my voice. And the people I loved.

∞

In *A Tale for the Time Being*, Ruth lies in bed with her husband, Oliver. She thinks, "What does separation look like? A wall? A wave? A body of water? A ripple of light or a shimmer of subatomic particles, parting?"

Or does it look like this: A locked steel door? A black eye? Addiction? A gun and a uniform? A mind that places a wall between you and the divine?

∞

After Greg's visit, I am depleted. I return to the cell. The deputy makes me wait while he takes his time unlocking it. When he pops the door, I step inside and Duckie says with no preamble, "God, there are so many hos in this place, screaming all over the place, 'My daddy this, my daddy that.' The girl in here before you was a ho, she stank. She wouldn't shut up."

"Uh-huh," I said, exhausted but too agitated to rest.

"Was there an election or something?" Duckie asked.

Come to think of it there was. Two days before I went in there were midterm elections in LA County. "Yes," I said. "How did you know?"

"They always round up the hos when there's an election or the president is coming to town or shit like that. Get the trash off the streets."

She sounded simultaneously disgusted with the prostitutes—would that include herself?—and the world at large that would treat people like eyesores and garbage.

About ten days into my sentence in Pregnant Dorm, I was called to the deputy's desk and was told I would be moving to Exit Dorm. Duckie had procured me a duffel bag, some extra thermals, and a couple more ibuprofen for my back pain, along with paper, a pencil, and her booking number so we could write when I got out. She also gave me her children's phone numbers.

"Call them," she said, crying. "Tell them I love them."

She sent me with her apples and her bran cereal—because she didn't eat anything that might be construed as healthy. She hugged me.

"Wait," she said. She reached under the bunk I slept in and pulled out one of her duffels. Inside was a brand-new blanket.

"Here," she said.

"I couldn't."

"I hear you shivering at night. I got this extra tire on me keeping me warm. Take it."

"Thank you," I said.

"Don't cry," she said.

Miss Jones gathered up two extra lunches.

"Here, baby, take these. You may be going home. But you may not be going for a while. So take the food. No telling when you'll eat again."

I was afraid. I didn't want to leave. What would happen to me? Who would I bunk with? Exit Dorm was general population: murderers, thieves, prostitutes, batterers, drunks, and addicts. And I loved Duckie. I loved Miss Jones. I had found safety there among the pregnant women and the few of us who had mysteriously landed there without being pregnant.

I was lined up with several other women also going to Exit Dorm. The deputy searched my duffel. He took my extra lunches that Miss Jones had given me and threw them away. He paused and looked at the books I had in my bag.

"These yours?"

I nodded.

"Why you wasting your time draggin' this shit around?"

I shrugged. *Keep quiet,* I whispered to myself. *Let him say what he wants. You are not what he thinks you are.*

"Go on," the deputy said as if disgusted that I had taken his time up with my books. As if reading insulted him. *Remember,* I told myself, *those in power despise knowledge.* "Hurry up. Get in line."

I started to walk away.

"Hurry. Jesus, you're slow. Hurry up."

I didn't look back to say good-bye to Duckie. I could hear Miss Jones crying. As I was marched along the red line to Exit Dorm, I remembered a passage in *A Tale for the Time Being* when Nao begins to understand the beauty of living:

> *A single moment is all we need to establish our human will and attain truth. . . . Both life and death manifest in every moment of existence. Our human body appears and disappears moment by moment, without cease, and this ceaseless arising and passing away is what we experience as time and being. They are not separate. They are one thing, and in even a fraction of a second, we have the opportunity to choose, and to turn the course of our action either toward the attainment of truth or away from it. Each instant is utterly critical to the whole world.*

CHAPTER FOUR

Exit Module

Louie was furious at the sharks. He thought that they had an understanding: The men would stay out of the shark's turf— the water—and the sharks would stay off theirs—the raft. He stewed all night, scowled hatefully at the sharks all day, and eventually made a decision. If the sharks were going to try to eat him, he was going to try to eat the sharks.

—Laura Hillenbrand, *Unbroken*

E xit Dorm is all shadow and darkness when I arrive. I am lined up with fourteen other women in front of the deputy's desk. I am not afraid, but I don't feel as if I am in my body. Later, someone suggests I was disassociating. I don't know. I know that my addiction was an attempt to achieve a state of numbness, because I had, my entire life, felt everything so acutely. I remember as a little girl thinking I could feel the blood flow through my veins. I remember tasting noise. Even beautiful music hurt my skin. And I felt the weight of the world's suffering. I couldn't even watch *Mutual of Omaha's Wild Kingdom*, a favorite of my alcoholic dad's in the 1970s, because animals had to kill each other to eat.

As my addiction progressed, from drinking and smoking weed on the weekends to every day at lunch in high school, then as much as possible in college, and so on, so, too, did the demoralization. The worse I felt about myself, the more I drank and used drugs to distance my heart from both the person I was becoming and the increasingly scary circumstances I placed myself in, from the hurts and abuses that I subjected myself to because of drink, risking my life and my dignity.

Now, standing in my fog of emptiness, my body floats above me. The deputy is taking her time. She is mean, meaner than the "po-lice" in Pregnant Dorm. Even though every module looks the same, the feeling of every module is different. Here I sense disorder. Crazy is in the air. I have twenty-seven days to go. My attorney told me I'd be out in four days. His promises to that effect, unmet and now, I realize, callously made, have ruined me. Duckie said I'd probably do 10 percent of my time. But now my hope that I will be a "10 percenter" has faded.

The deputy finally gets to me.

"Upper tier, forty-eight."

I now know where that is, so I take my roll-up and my duffel and head up the stairs. The women in Dayroom are moving around, watching, but most are asleep. I don't know what time it is, but it must be around 3 or 4 a.m. I climb the stairs and hear the door to Cell 48 pop. I walk inside and am immediately freaked out.

The cell is a pigsty. There are soiled towels on the ground. The tiny window is covered with paper. Both bunks are loaded down with crap. Clothing hangs everywhere. Books line the little desk and across the sill near the window. It stinks to high heaven. A dodgy, skin-and-bones meth addict stands up. I will learn later that the Department of Children and Family Services (DCFS) has taken her kids. While she is here, she will lose custody of them and they will be adopted out.

Something about her—I don't like her on sight. Why do I reserve my compassion for only those I deem worthy of it?

I stand there. Then I say, "There's no way I'm living in this shit."

She looks mean, but for whatever reason, she is cowed by me. She must be afraid now of losing her privacy. Barely anyone gets a cell to herself, and I can see why she doesn't have a bunkie. Her sloth is manifest. My heart is beating fast.

"You need to uncover that window," I say. "And get those books off the desk. And what the fuck is with these wet rags on the ground? It's a cesspool in here."

She has been sleeping on the bottom bunk.

"And I'm restricted to bottom bunk," I say. "So you're gonna need to move that pile of shit to the top."

It's my fear turning me into a convict, I tell myself. *This isn't you.*

She starts to take the books down.

The methhead is white. Her hair is white. Her rabbit eyes look pink. Her eyebrows are white. I long for Duckie and her El Eme tats, her big ass, her pickles and eggs. I want to hear her sing. I'd even take the snoring over this.

I stand there, still holding my roll-up. I don't want to put it down anywhere. MRSA, a staph infection, is rampant in jails. I am afraid of contracting it, though when I saw my doctor before coming to Lynwood, he told me not to worry. If I contracted it, it was easily treatable.

"Not in a jail," I told him. "They don't treat you in jail."

"You'll be home soon, Leslie," he said. "Don't worry."

The methhead is moving around, taking things off the walls. I can't believe the stuff is even on the walls. Why has this lesion been allowed to fester? In Pregnant Dorm, one woman got the hole for not removing a poster from her wall. Unlike this woman, she was African American.

After a while, the methhead goes out to the catwalk, the balcony surrounding upper tier.

"Miss," she shouts down. "Deputy, this girl is harassing me. I'm afraid of her. She is threatening to hurt me."

"You little bitch," I say.

"She's calling me names."

I can't believe this is happening. I'm gonna end up in the hole. They'll extend my sentence. They can do this. I have a release date and an extended release date, just in case I fuck up. Shit. Shit.

But it doesn't happen. All of sudden, the methhead is packing up. She's leaving.

"Bitch," she says to me. "Lucky for me, I got Dayroom because you're such a cunt."

"Fine, leave, get out."

She packs up and leaves. The cell is still putrid. Obviously, the windows don't open in jail so I'm not sure what to do about the smell. She has left her wet towels on the floor. Trash is everywhere, and I am stuck cleaning it up. But at last there is no one to bother me. Relief swells. Then comes fear. Who will I talk to? I can't be alone. When I'm alone, there is only time. I've already read all four books that I've received.

That's when Johnnie shows up, holding her roll-up. She is a tall, beautiful woman. I can imagine her walking around with a crown on her head, like a queen. But she has a scowl of hatred on her face. I notice that most of the black women in jail look at me with a scowl on their faces. There's not a lot of racial politics in Lynwood—in a way it feels harder to get along amid the anger on the streets of Los Angeles than in Lynwood—but it doesn't mean you don't feel it sometimes. This woman's scowl seems to be related to the cell. I can tell she thinks I'm the one who turned the space into a toxic landfill. She looks at me with disgust.

See, I say to myself, *your Karma is quick. Only moments ago, you did the same to that poor, childless methhead.*

"Mmm, mmm, mmm, mmm, mmm," she says, melodically. She shakes her head. She is already done with me.

"I didn't do this shit," I say.

She gazes at me as if I am nothing.

"I just moved into this," I say. "It's that blond methhead down there."

Nothing. Just a look that wants me dead. But it doesn't even land. I have only two fears: The Death of Time and Being Alone. Everything else—gravy.

"Fine. You can stand there staring at me or you can help me clean this up," I say.

"I don't want to put my roll-up down anywhere."

"Welcome to the club," I say.

We start to clean the mess. I am so disgusted I want to puke. I keep thinking, *This is the moment I contract MRSA.*

"What's your name?" I say.

"Johnnie."

"I'm Leslie."

"Hmmph."

Okaaay, I think. *Fun, fun, fun.*

So far, four books have arrived: *Alcoholics Anonymous, The Collected Poems of Mary Oliver, A Tale for the Time Being*, and *All the Light We Cannot See. All the Light We Cannot See* is gloriously long. This should take a week at least, I think with glee.

And indeed, I read it as if I were counting snowflakes. Slowly, with a luxuriousness that bathed me. The book made me feel weightless. It almost ruined my eyes. At night, the deputies turned down the lights—never off, just down—but I had a galactic case of insomnia so I read the book beneath the brown wash of haze that filtered from the dimmed nightlights above. I kept telling myself as I read it, *Slow down, slow down.* To make it last, I would often close the book and gaze longingly at that beautiful cover. Sometimes I could hear the tide swell and close in on little Saint-Malo. The book, the cover, the dreams and yearning it inspired in me, turned down the prattle in my head, the constant screaming deputies, the sounds of countless toilets flushing over and over and over again. Sometimes my experience with it was so bittersweet that I'd have to put it aside, to ease my melancholy and my yearning. When I saw that Doerr's masterpiece was moving too fast, I would get scared. What will I do when it's over? Should I skip parts so that I am forced to read it again? But alas, in two days, I was finished.

I was furious at Greg for sending the *AA Big Book*. I implored him when he dropped me off not to send it because as I waited and waited to surrender, I saw a woman dragging a cart of books into the jail that contained Bibles and *Big Book*s exclusively. He sent it anyway, possibly afraid I might relapse. Anyone who knows anything about jail knows that drugs are available. Lynwood, I will learn, is no exception. I would rather die than relapse, I told him. But I had said those words to him a thousand times before and always relapsed.

I only understood his choice later. Fearful I'd slip, the book must have felt to him like insurance against disaster. In my cell, staring at the book, I fumed. A wasted book in my three-a-week allotment. It made me think of that *Twilight Zone* episode where the end of the world has come. Only one man survives. He's a nerd who loves to read. He finds himself on the steps of the New York City Public Library, gleeful and happy. All those millions of books to read. He can't believe his luck.

Then he breaks his glasses.

I remember placing the *Big Book* tenderly into my duffel but feeling, at the same time, that awful alcoholicky, selfishy frustration of not getting my way.

My new bunkie and I throw the towels outside the cell. (Inmates call their cells their "rooms," something I refuse to do.) We rip down the paper that the tweaker put up over the window. I have a view this time; not of other windows of other cells, but of the 105 Freeway and the projects across the street.

We go through the books she's left behind: tawdry paperbacks, Bibles of every form and variety, pamphlets about addiction, and scrap heaps of court papers. Johnnie starts to rip up the court documents.

"Wait," I say. "Maybe we should give them to her."

"Who, Bubbles out there?"

I laugh. I will come to see that Johnnie gives everyone a nickname.

"She might want them."

"She a dumb bitch."

"That might be true, but still . . ."

She looks at me like *what the hell?* Then she shrugs.

"I ain't giving 'em to her," she says.

"I'll do it."

I get that raised eyebrow look again.

I take the papers, put them in my duffel. I will give them to Bubbles when I program, which could be a day away, two hours away, sixteen hours away, in the next five minutes. The "po-lice" lording over us don't observe a schedule. It's just another way of fucking with us. And if anyone acts out, we don't program at all.

"Acting out," to them, has many definitions. For instance—if an inmate presses the emergency button, that could cause a lockdown. You would think that might elicit concern rather than their ire, but deputies hate the emergency button because lots of women press it. Sometimes inmates press it just to mess things up, boredom and stifled rage being the predecessor to chaos. Sometimes, it's an accident. The 911 button is located just above the toilet flush button and looks almost identical. On my first day, I accidentally pressed it after using the toilet. I thought it was the flush button. (Why the fuck did they put those two identical buttons one on top of the other? It made no sense. But then again, that's jail.) Sometimes it *is* an emergency, but because they never checked on you when you pressed the emergency button, it could evolve into a full-blown crisis. I was told numerous times about the women who died or were seriously injured because a deputy did not respond to the emergency button. I saw that blatant disregard more than once. I remember one day, a young woman had a seizure during program. It took deputies an hour to mobilize. Eventually they tossed her on a furniture dolly and hauled her out like a broken desk.

Johnnie and I have put the cell back into order. I am relieved by increments. She still gives me that look, but at least I know she is, like me, uncharitable toward filth. And she doesn't smell, a constant bunkie complaint in jail for obvious reasons. Duckie was no sachet pillow. Like me, Johnnie seems to value her hygiene in a place where staying clean is challenging. And she *is* beautiful. I love looking at her.

"How old are you?" I ask. I can't tell. She is world-aged. She has seen the darkness. You can tell.

"Twenty-one."

She hasn't reciprocated much in our conversation thus far. But this time, she says, "You look pretty old."

"Wow, those are some amazing friend skills you got there. Teach me your secrets."

She looks at me. A beat . . . then we are laughing our heads off.

"I'm old enough to be your mother," I say.

She makes a face. "Let's get this shit out of here," she says.

I am grateful the deputy hasn't locked our door yet as we clean. So we take the towels gingerly and haul them downstairs.

"Don't put those there," the deputy says.

"Well then, what should we do with them?" Johnnie asks. She is insolent with her knife-throwing sweet voice. I am impressed. I would never talk like that to a deputy, never use that tone of voice. That's partly why I ended up in here, after all.

"I don't care what you do with them, just don't put them there," the deputy said with the usual disgust and hatred for us.

Johnnie and I look at each other. Once again, because of a deputy, a silent alliance has formed. If what they're looking for is control, they are deluded. My new bunkie remembers our common enemy. We don't roll our eyes, because we've both learned how to roll our eyes without rolling our eyes. We walk the moist MRSA-carrying towels and the bags of trash back upstairs and leave them outside our door.

"Close the door, forty-eight," the deputy shouts.

"Bitch," Johnnie says.

The door is closed, the lock clicks. It's just me and the queen now.

I'm despairing of having nothing to read. One of the many anxieties that goes along with moving around the modules is that the mail gets hung up. Letters take a while to catch up. So do books. My husband says three more are on the way. But what if they *never* come? In jail I use words like "never," "always," "forever." They pollute my vocabulary. And now with my mostly hostile bunkie, I have no means of escape. It will be hell *forever and ever*, I think. I will *never* get another book again and my pain will *always* be with me.

One day I receive a letter from Duckie. Obviously there's no "inter-jail mail," but evidently they don't mind if you send a letter through regular means. I imagine the letter's journey. It starts in the jail mailroom, where they open and read every letter. When it passes muster they stamp the word "Inspected" on the outside, then slap a piece of tape over the once-sealed envelope. The letter that originated from Duckie then departs for the nearby US Postal Service processing center, where it is separated, barcoded, and sorted by size and zip code. I imagine it after that on the truck, with all the other bundles of mail, heading for the local post office, where it is sorted again, placed in another mailbag with thousands of other pieces of mail, and sent back to Lynwood. Once at Lynwood, it's taken to the jail processing station, opened, read, stamped "Inspected" again, then sorted and sent to me. All of this, and she is just one floor above me.

My first thought when I look at the envelope, torn open twice and double stamped, sloppily taped, a near ruination of a letter, is that Duckie used one of her precious stamps to send it to me. It is then that I fully understand her. Why she did what she did for me: the brand-new underwear, arranging my release for church with the trustees, the ibuprofens, the blanket, the duffel bag. Duckie's soul—her basic self—is a generous self. A loving self. To her very core, Duckie is a charitable and bighearted woman. I try to imagine what her life would have been like had she not been rendered into her condition by the poverty, neglect, and violence that fueled her addiction. What gifts would she have given to the world?

I read the letter slowly, trying my best to make it last.

> *My new friend, Leslie . . . don't worry about the past,*
> *just handle life one day at a time and know there is a*
> *God and he has your plan all worked out already.*

How I wished I could believe that. How I wished I had her faith.

> *Bless your heart and bless you always . . . I'm here and*
> *don't know how to get back on track because I was*
> *robbed of my babies.*

I realized that the loss of her children, who were wrested from her not by the county, but the Mafia way, was the thing that finally destroyed her. I knew Duckie had huge plans for her release: sobriety, new teeth, a job. But I feared that the hole inside her was too big. Once delivered to the streets without money or housing or clean clothes, no food, no education, and a fierce addict nature, I saw the reality of the odds stacked against her.

One foot in front of the other, she wrote, *and go do your thing*

*like only you can!!! Shine. I'll be waiting to hear from you. Thank
you for everything. God be with you in all you do. I love your life,
Love and respect, Vanessa.*

∞

The books arrive on Tuesday: *Unbroken, One Hundred Years of
Solitude, A History of Loneliness.* The titles alone are like a three-
line poem about my life. Johnnie looks at them.

"Are you depressed or something?"

"What?" I say. "You're not?"

I had already read Márquez's masterpiece, but it had been a
long time. And the book wasn't depressing in the least. *A History
of Loneliness* was about a priest in Ireland, the sex scandal. I was
curious about shame at the time. I never finished it. As for *Unbroken*, I never wanted to read it. That's why it made the list. I
figured boredom would force me to capitulate. My choices struck
me as curious. Why, I wondered, these books? With all the
books in the world, why these? I try to remember what my
thinking was when I put the list together for Greg. I know there
were books I wanted to read, and some I wanted to read again.
Maybe some of them were recommended to me, but those days
before Lynwood are almost like a blackout. I can see myself writing the list, scratching books out, adding others, retyping it. But
there seems to be no logic to my choices. What I know is that
the books are beginning to show up when I need them. Each one

the most important temporal lesson I need, just when I need it. It is as if a hand juts through the jailhouse roof above over and over again, to dispense every book, even the ones that seem weirdly chosen, exactly when I need them.

I have always been an avid reader, ever since I can remember. I was one of *those* kids who chose long afternoons in my bedroom reading, over the hot summer days of fun and play. To my mom's credit—she had a lot of problems—but that woman, bless her, brought my two brothers and me to the library every two weeks when we were kids. Going to the library was like having a birthday twice a month. Borrowing books? Who ever heard of such an idea? It was the best idea anyone had ever come up with as far as I was concerned. When we got home, I would take the books—you could check out only three at a time—and lay them out on my bed. The choice of where to start was blissful agony. The best hurt in the world. Once the choice was made, I'd devour them. Two weeks couldn't come quick enough. Books were fickle, like love. They were my early boyfriends. They created in my brain the same rush that sex and drugs and music did later. I loved holding them in my hands before reading them. And later when I started amassing and collecting books, I never lent them to people. I am not generally selfish with my stuff—in fact, my tendency is to be generous to a fault, most especially with my time; for students, alcoholics, and addicts who need help, my friends and family. I am also free with my money. To the consternation of many, I hand it out to homeless people frequently, most often to the worst drunks and addicts. "They're just going to use it for alcohol" is the snarky refrain I hear repeatedly. "So?" I answer back. But books; those are the one thing no one gets. I just build more shelves in my house to store them.

I laid the three books out on my metal slab. I had read that Laura Hillenbrand, author of *Unbroken*, suffered from chronic fatigue, and it manifested in dizziness. She told the *New York Times* that she always felt like she was on a ship, rolling around. After she had to leave college because of the disease, she lost contact with all her friends. People didn't believe her, even her own mother.

"When almost everyone in your world is looking down on you and condemning you for bad behavior, it's very hard not to let that point of view envelop you, until you start to feel terrible about yourself. I just began to feel such deep shame, because I was the target of so much contempt," she told the reporter at the *Times*.

I never forgot that. It was the main reason I wanted to read the book: not because it was a bestseller, not because one day it would be a movie, not because everyone loved it. It was the author and her struggle that made me want to read it. She was sick, and people didn't believe she had a "real" disease. I related to that and to her battles with a disease that even her closest allies thought she should have had the moral toughness to "get over." Because people told me, like they did her, if I just used my will, if I was just stronger, better, nicer, calmer, etc., I'd get "over" my addiction. I understood her shame. But more than that, she wrote this amazing book *in spite of being dizzy all the time*. I had to see how she did it under that duress.

In jail, you think the weirdest thoughts. I remember thinking I would rather be in jail for thirty-seven days than be dizzy all the time. I still think this. Which makes me admire Hillenbrand even more. I can put the symptoms of addiction—using and drinking and going to jail—into remission. She has to live with her condition every day. All the time.

The story of *Unbroken* is pretty straightforward. As a boy, Louis "Louie" Zamperini is a chronic troublemaker. His older brother steps in and encourages him to channel all that raw energy into running. It turns out Louis is a good runner. He later qualifies for the 1936 Olympics. When World War II breaks out, Louie, like almost everyone, enlists in the military. His plane crashes in the Pacific and amazingly he survives forty-seven days adrift in a raft, until his capture by the Japanese navy. Being a prisoner is in no way better than starving to death on a raft. Louie becomes the favorite target of a particularly vicious prison commander and nearly starves to death. His time in the POW camp is unparalleled for its intense cruelty. If I could sum the book up in a word, I'd say it was about survival: mental, spiritual, and physical.

Two things about Louie Zamperini. First, he survived six weeks and five days in shark-infested waters with cunning and a human fortitude I'd never before read about. *Forty-seven* days. I only had thirty-seven days locked up, and it was a lot easier. For instance, even if it was barely edible, I still had food, and even though it had holes in it, I still had a blanket. Two, actually, thanks to Duckie's generosity. And, second, unlike Louie, I had already done my battle with death, having been revived two separate times during my relapse. My sharks were just men and women in sausage-skin sheriff's uniforms, and not very smart ones at that. Louie's sharks wanted to eat him.

In one scene, which I will never forget as long as I live, the men who survived the plane crash over the Pacific and ended up on the raft—Louie, Mac, and Phil—were drifting close to death when Louie noticed the sharks were gone. This was odd.

> *Never in four weeks had the sharks left. Louie got up on his knees and leaned out over the water, looking as far down as he could, puzzled.*
>
> *He was kneeling there, perched over the edge of the raft, when one of the sharks that he had touched leapt from the water at terrific speed, mouth wide open, lunging straight at his head.*

What follows is two paragraphs of a heart-stopping epic battle where Mac and Louie use their oars to fight the sharks back. The way I read it, it seemed like the sharks that had been circling them for a month decided they had to figure out a better strategy for eating Louie and his two companions. I remember picturing them under the ocean, sitting at a card table, bottles of whiskey littered about, cigarettes burning in ashtrays. (No, none of this makes sense, but stay with me.) They talk it out, their shark voices super gangster. Then they come up with their plan. They will take turns jumping out of the water and grabbing the men one by one and eating them.

The one thing the sharks didn't count on was that these men had a primal urge to live. They were resilient. They wanted to go home, to breathe the air of the places where they grew up, to see their parents, their girlfriends. They weren't trying to be heroes. They were trying to save their lives.

How many times had I tried to save my life? The count is excessive. And yet I could never do it. My addiction had a hold on me. Then something happened. Somehow I made it to a rehab in Santa Fe, New Mexico, five days after my last arrest. I arrived out of my mind and was secured in Cabin 10, the detox cabin. It was not willpower that stopped me. If I had willpower, I wouldn't have relapsed in the first place. I wouldn't have used drugs and alcohol at all, starting as a child. What non-addicts simply do not understand—and it's reasonable that they don't—is that no human power, not mine, not the police's, not the doctor's, not the rehab "specialist's," could stop me. Only surrender could stop me. That split second of grace. One time post-Lynwood, I explained my experience of this gift to a room of sober people. "It was like a window that opened, but would only stay open for a millisecond," I said. "And a random puff of wind blew me through it."

Cabin 10 was notorious. It was the place they put the incorrigible and deathly ill, the suicide risks and the patients on the list for coding out. I met all four criteria and was assigned a minder who sat with me 24-7 for forty-eight hours. Susan, a wrinkled, kind lady—think Aunt Bee from *The Andy Griffith Show*—attended me. That was her job. The entire time, I couldn't believe anyone would take a job like that. She was so nice and she drove me so crazy. She talked nonstop, stories about her daughter and her dog and her sister and her house. Today, I see her ceaseless rambling for what it really was—an act of love. Anything to keep me distracted from the seizure-like DTs, the hallucinations, and the sickness. Nevertheless, for those two days, I wanted nothing more than for her to shut up. To just let me die. I didn't know at that point the degree to which I had destroyed my life, only that I was very sick and likely in big trouble.

That I stayed sober surprised almost everyone. When I left Life Healing Center, my favorite caregiver there, a woman I called Commando because she wore fatigues and combat boots (and did prison time), couldn't even say good-bye to me. She was skeptical of my sobriety and had someone send me a note that said, "If I see you, I'll cry. I will pray for you every day." I loved her fiercely. She had an incontrovertible part in saving my life.

When I called her two years after I'd been released from jail to ask her about what I had been like in rehab, she said, "To be honest, I am shocked you're still clean. You did not want to get sober. When you left us, you were not ready to deal with the inside stuff. I didn't think you would make it."

"Well, here I am, calling you, sober," I said.

I could hear her weeping. "Hold on a sec," she said. "I'm having a Hallmark moment."

What she didn't know, and in a way, I didn't know either

until much later, was that at that rehab I had a profound, fundamental change. One night, I woke up out of two days and nights of hallucinations and looked out the window to see a crescent moon in the sky surrounded by stars. Susan was sitting there quietly watching me as I labored through the potentially fatal occupation of detoxing liquor and drugs. I distinctly remember her silhouette in the darkness against what felt like an overly bright shaft of moonlight.

Everything seemed to stop. The moon was wavering out the window, almost like it was being held loosely on the branch of a tree. I couldn't be sure if I was still hallucinating, but I could clearly see the dark sky and the play of planetary light. I thought it was beautiful and I wondered where the moon had gone in the past year and seven weeks of my relapse when I had been in a constant blackout. I had no recollection of seeing the moon or the stars in ages. *Hello, moon,* I said. *Where have you been for the last year?* It was then, out of the blue, that the thought came to me that I should stop looking for happiness. That it was the pursuit of happiness, and professional and material success, that had deposited me right there in the center of my hell in Santa Fe, New Mexico. Somehow I knew that what I needed in order to survive was to learn, *really* learn, how to stop thinking about myself and to love, *really love*, other people.

I don't know why I had this moment of awareness, but it became infinitely clear to me that if I was going to live through this and all future indignities—I had no idea at that moment how horrible my life was about to become; that one day I would be going to jail because of my wreckage—then I would have to find some way to mitigate my affliction and the anguish it had caused. And somehow I understood this to mean that I would have to search for something else in life, something that would transcend my slavish devotion to immediate gratification and the worldly acquisition of stuff, particularly the preservation of my career and the capitulation to my ego. Except for the moon, everything around me was dark and I was terrified. It didn't last long, but I suspect it was the first time in my life I'd experienced an awakening, the transcendence of myself.

Louie sat in that boat, furious. Fucking sharks. He didn't say that, but I did. I hated them, and it's a testament to Hillenbrand's evocative writing, her wry, crafty humor, that swept me up into Louie's dilemma. He decided, "If the sharks were going to try to eat him, he was going to try to eat them."

What followed was a hilariously told story about his plan to beat the sharks at their own game. His initial attempt nearly killed him. The plan was weak, by his own admission. He had leaned over and grabbed the tail of a big shark. That was a mistake. The shark beelined for the water, with Louie attached, and when it hit, the wave sent water up Louie's nose and into his mouth, nearly drowning him. He got back onto the raft, with no memory of how he had done so.

The thought of starting smaller occurred to him. Take the

enemy in increments and defeat him slowly over time. He and Phil worked together, dangling bait, luring the shark, and then Louie grabbed the creature around the tail and dragged it into the raft. Moving quickly, Phil smashed the flare cartridge into the shark's mouth while Louie used the pliers to stab the screwdriver end into the boneless monster's eyes. The shark's death was instantaneous.

So it is with addiction. In the first thirty days, when all you can think about is simultaneously giving up or staying the course—an agonizing medley of urges—you do what Louie did. You take a sharp object and you plunge it into all your old ideas about your monsters. And then you eat them.

When I read that, I felt brave. I knew that all the sharks in the world could not take me down anymore. They could journey with me, but I had a choice; and once I'd made my decision to try something else, to seek out spiritual answers for my problems, I never had to invite them on board again. The thing I learned in recovery, which was confirmed for me in jail—and that Hillenbrand so eloquently and metaphorically detailed about Louie's experience—is that the monsters are always there. But we survive in spite of them because we know they have no power over us unless we give it to them.

∞

It turns out Johnnie and I like each other and can make each other laugh. I am relieved she is smart, and I enjoy how rogue and scabrous her humor is. One day she and I are sitting around in our cell, falling under the torpid weight of boredom. I decide to get a conversation going. Anything to push back death by tedium.

"So, Johnnie . . ."

Her eyes soften. She is so incredibly young when she softens. So beautiful.

"Johnnie's my ho name," she says.

"Why do you call yourself a ho? That's . . . it's awful."

"Because I *am* a ho."

"Jesus," I say. "So what's your real name, then?"

It was as if she were confessing some shameful thing, and it made me very sad.

"Wynell."

"Well, thanks for telling me. I hated that I called you by your 'ho' name."

"Wynell is a boy's name," she says.

It wasn't a huge mystery why someone—someone whose otherness had always been part of her American experience—would change her name, but it intrigued me that she had chosen a boy's name for her street identity, when she was also embarrassed that her given name had a masculine feel. But people adopt new names for all kinds of reasons. They are an assertion of belonging, but one of exclusion, too. I once read that nineteenth-century writer Nathaniel Hawthorne added the "w" to his name to distance himself from his family's involvement in the Salem witch trials, most especially his relation to John Hathorne. Hathorne was the only judge involved in the trials who did not apologize for his part in the deaths of innocents, probably because apologizing meant he'd have to admit he was wrong.

Once Wynell told me her real name, I began to see the island in our friendship. When Duckie gave me the exclusive right to use her street name, we were family. When Wynell told me her given name, we were friends. I was touched that I had experienced this trust. Over time, she became my best friend in Lynwood.

One day out of the blue she said, "I hate white girls."

Not even a second passed. "I don't hate black girls. Except you for saying that."

We howled. Hysterical laughter.

Wynell's world of "ho-ing," as the prostitutes called their livelihood, was a world I knew nothing about. My feelings for Wynell grew to pure love when I learned about the horrors in her life, and the daily struggle she faced, her choice of companions, and the tragedy of her impossible upbringing. She had been locked up five times by the age of twenty-one, a truth that devastated me.

Tough, wise Wynell taught me how to do my time by losing her patience with me. It happened like this: One day as I stood by the window fuming because they weren't letting us out to program *again*, she said to me, "Girl, you got to learn to do your time. You are going to make me crazy with your crazy-ass motherfucking crazy-lady noises over there by that door. You ain't in here alone and you are fucking with my serenity."

For whatever reason, I heard that. I am not sure how, but that day I accepted fully and without reservation the four walls in the eight-by-ten cell I shared with Wynell. They never again felt like they were closing in on me. I still hated them, but, of course, you don't have to allow that which you hate to lord over you. I was grateful to her for leveling with me and making no bones about how I was fucking up her tranquility.

She and I stayed up late laughing every night, recapping our favorite episodes from the TV show *The First 48*. Both of us, ironically, loved this police procedural and, it turned out, both of us knew every detail of every episode we shared with each other. Talking about the different stories was almost like watching TV, only more fun because we each added our own opinions or acted out various scenes, making detective and gangster voices. Wynell was hilarious and generous with her impressions, especially of the criminals. And it occurred to me then how powerful our memory and imagination can be when they need to be. *No one needs TV,* I thought one night after we'd exhausted ourselves telling stories. We have our brains and the capacity not just to reiterate narrative but to make it come alive as we go along.

She had not yet told me everything about her life—that would come over time—but the little details she let loose showed me that she was tough. Wynell was a woman who ran the streets, took rape as a matter of course, drowned her sorrows with E&J (good old Easy Jesus), and when she wasn't living with a drunken, sallow sixty-five-year-old man, worked her nights in flea-infested motels turning tricks. But for every time she was hard and cold and mean, I saw moments of great vulnerability. I was surprised the first time she cried; I began to love her like she was my daughter.

One day, a prostitute that Wynell knew from where they turned tricks came by our cell. Cookie was a trustee. She and Wynell would joke around at the door all the time. But Cookie was crazy. She must have had ADHD, which I think so many of the women inside suffer from. And if Wynell hated white girls, Cookie's eyes blazed with rage toward me.

That day, Cookie was angling for a new bunkie. She was about to get locked up in a cell because she was too disruptive in Dayroom. She came to the door.

"Hey, J, leave that white girl. Come bunk with me."

Wynell laughed.

"Come on, girl, I don't want some bitch in there with me."

"Nah," Wynell said.

Cookie couldn't believe it. "Oh, are you *lez-be-ans?*"

"Get the fuck out. I ain't moving," Wynell said.

"Serious? You gonna stay with that?"

"Yeah, I'm staying with her."

It was so strange to see Cookie turn and walk away, all her bravado sunk. And it was a shock to me—and a relief—that Wynell turned one of her homegirls away for the old white lady she was currently bunking with.

I know that I found our time locked up together peaceful. I

think she did, too, but I can't ever be 100 percent sure. She wore some things close. Yet, every day, she would get up, stand by the window, and say, "I am at peace because I choose to be at peace," to which I would reply, "Shut the fuck up."

One time, she came to the cell fuming. She'd been getting into it with this crazy inmate for days, brooding over the way the woman kept asking for her food and taunting her, as if to get into it with her.

"I am gonna beat that bitch down."

And she really was. I said, "Wynell, you can't do that. You are crying every night to get out of here."

She wouldn't let go. Her anger was so dog-on-a-mailman.

I spent ten minutes talking her down. I said, "You can't reason with the untreated mentally ill."

I don't know why that was the one argument I had that she was able to hear. I suppose all of us inside had known crazy on an intimate level—addiction does that to you, but so does a traumatic upbringing. Maybe it is wrong for me to talk about "us" in a general way, but I came to know that whatever the circumstances of our individual upbringing, there was among us collectively a sense of not knowing how to be regular people. As if all our lives we had been parroting "normal," though we desperately wanted to *be* normal.

From then on, following any encounter with the crazy inmate, Wynell just turned and walked away from her. I was glad because Wynell had a temper and I wanted her to get out as much as she herself wanted to get out. We all had two release dates; our state-sanctioned release date and a later one in case you earned more time for bad behavior while locked up. One trip to solitary could mean a longer sentence. But in all honesty, I can admit that my pleas to her were also of a selfish nature. My fear of time in jail was eclipsed only by my fear of being alone doing time with myself in jail. I did not want her to be sent away. I already knew that her release date was a week earlier than mine and whenever I thought of that, I would panic.

"Please don't do anything to get into trouble," I would say. "I don't want to be left behind. Please." I like to think that she also heard that plea, that it motivated her somehow, as arrogant as that seems. But I know that Wynell had a big heart. She liked to pretend she didn't, but it was there.

More so than being alone, I didn't want a different bunkie because, while I had been lucky so far, there were *truly* difficult women in there. Violent women. Women who really did need lockup, especially in the absence of mental health services. Some, it seemed, were well beyond sanity and I was glad they were not free. One trustee, Miss Mouse, was in for cutting her drug connect up into itty-bitty pieces.

During this segment of my incarceration, Duckie ended up in Exit Dorm. She had fought with someone at the water faucet and was moved out of Pregnant Dorm shortly thereafter.

"I took a broom and beat her around the head," she told me. Something about self-defense.

I was amazed that Duckie wasn't in lockdown. She wasn't taking her meds, she said, but selling them for food on commissary and cash for her release. When she got out, she said, there would be no shelter, no food, no clean clothes. But now, without her meds, she was unraveling. And I saw for the first time the repetitive nature of homelessness and addiction, and the cycles of madness and sanity that went with it. Poverty, I realized, led people to impossible choices, trading whatever slim mental health options they had for money to eat or a place to stay. Still, I had two friends there now, even though Wynell hated Duckie.

"She ain't got your best interests at heart," Wynell told me.

In jail small things were hurtful and perceived attentions given to one person over another made for jealousy. I understood and said nothing.

Every night, when we ran out of *First 48* episodes, Wynell and I would take turns reading to each other. Wynell loved and hated the horrible parts of *Unbroken*. They definitely had that car crash quality to them: look, but don't *watch*. Other times, I would read passages that felt absolutely real to me in my experience locked up. They affected her, too, sometimes with outbursts of disgust, other times with silence.

There was one particular passage that spoke to the dignity it requires to stay alive. Even if the body wants to give up, Hillenbrand writes, it is access to that dignity that sustains prisoners and keeps them alive. It seemed true for Louie. It seemed true, too, for people like Viktor Frankl and Elie Wiesel, who survived the Holocaust, and Harriet Tubman, whose worthy acts dignified her and gave her a reason to live. In slavery and oppression, Hillenbrand seems to say, the difference between living and dying is the preservation of dignity.

Though I can't compare my experience in county jail with the experience of slaves and Holocaust victims, or Louie's and Phil's experience in the Japanese POW camp, I could certainly relate to the issue of dignity. Everything inside Lynwood was designed to strip you of your self-esteem. Everything. But there were always acts of quiet resistance. We would give the guards names: Wolf Eyes, Bologna, K-Won, Grim Reaper, and Stick. The inmates would "cheek" their meds at pill call for others who couldn't get pain medication or laxatives. Since the guards called us ladies (when they weren't also calling us insects), we called ourselves and each other bitches. As in "Yo, bitch, can I have your cereal if you don't want it?" Wynell liked to "fall" from her bunk so she would have to go to medical for her "injuries" just to change things up. At least once a week, someone clogged their toilet to get out of their cell. Ingenuity was the safeguard of dignity.

The same was true for Louie. Hillenbrand writes: "Louie soon learned a critical rule of conversation: Never use a guard's real name. Guards who discovered they were being discussed often delivered savage beatings, so the men invented nicknames for them . . . Turdbird, Flange, Face, the Weasel."

There were other acts of defiance at Louie's POW camp. Hilarious ones. Sometimes they would save up all their farts—chronic dysentery made them especially ripe—and when told to bow before the emperor, they "would pitch forward in concert and let thunderclaps fly for Hirohito." One POW convinced a guard that he could make a sundial work at night by lighting a match. Louie began keeping a diary with a stolen pencil and a tiny book that a fellow POW, a bookbinder in real life, had made for him out of rice paper. Louie would faintly write his entries upside down on the other side of pages that he filled with decoy writing—seemingly innocuous names and addresses. Then he hid the diary under a board in his cell. "With daily room inspections, discovery was likely, and would probably bring a clubbing. But this small declaration of self mattered a great deal to Louie. He knew that he might well die here. He wanted to leave a testament to what he had endured, and who he had been."

I loved Louie for taking the risk. Writing under the weight of censorship, and in this case possible death, was a profound act of a courage. Writing is survival. Leaving behind your testimony defies mortality. It pledges your allegiance to freedom. It saves you.

One day, Wynell found Maya Angelou's *I Know Why the Caged Bird Sings* in the "library." When you found a good book there, it was almost like finding gold in an old forty-niner creek bed.

You knew good books existed, but you figured you'd never see one again. Once in a while, someone would go home and leave her books behind and the women would swarm the "library." In moments, the pile would be picked clean. Wynell had found a treasure when she stumbled upon Angelou's book.

Angelou's book is one of the top ten most banned books in the United States. Since 1983, *I Know Why the Caged Bird Sings* has been publicly challenged thirty-nine times, even in my home state, liberal California. In 1982, at the American Booksellers Association, the book was displayed in a miniature prison cell for the inaugural Banned Books Week for the organization. It seemed fitting, then, that I was hearing it for the first time in jail.

Each night, after I read some of *Unbroken*, Wynell would share parts of Maya Angelou's memoir. "She don't like white people, I'm warning you."

"C'mon, Wynell, you can't keep putting me in your categories. Not all white people fly Confederate flags and carry a noose in the trunk of their cars."

"I'm sorry," she said. "I just . . ."

What she didn't say hung in the air. I knew the words. In fact, Maya Angelou expressed them beautifully in her book.

"'In Stamps the segregation was so complete that most Black children didn't really, absolutely know what whites looked like,'" Wynell read from *I Know Why the Cages Bird Sings*. "'Other than that they were different, to be dreaded, and in that dread was included the hostility of the powerless against the powerful, the poor against the rich, the worker against the worked for and the ragged against the well dressed. I remember never believing that whites were really real.'"

After Wynell read that, I sighed, but I couldn't find any way to articulate how sad it was to hear those words. I have never been able to understand how people can enslave other people. Or kill them because of the way they look or the god they worship. It is not beyond my comprehension that there are Hitlers and Trumps in the world. Evil exists. I saw some of that in jail. But what I don't understand is that evil has followers. That whites, for Angelou, were phantasmagorical, unreal, is a heartbreaking fallout of hatred. I couldn't say anything to Wynell, because I feared it would just sound like empty words. What I thought was that even animals don't *hate* each other. Only human beings hate.

I only had to look around me and see the reality of imprisonment. I was almost wholly surrounded by black and brown women, and of the few white women, most were uneducated and impoverished addicts. Why was that? It seemed to me that little had changed since slavery and indentured servitude; that it was only the *rules* of enslavement that had changed. The dominant culture—in our country that would be white males—just got smarter in its attempt to silence the critique of racism by hiding it better. Incarceration, homelessness, lack of health care, wage inequity, and bias and discrimination in education: these are the tenets of modern slavery. It lives on, but in an institutionalized way that people can choose not to see. It's easy to turn away from reality when it hurts too much to see the truth of our own hatred. It pained me to see that I was in the strictest minority in jail, and yet I knew so many, many white people who never served time for crimes that were worse than Wynell's, including the chronic criminal problem of white cops murdering unarmed black citizens. The seemingly endless injustice in our country and the helplessness I felt—that I could do little to change it—made me feel haunted and powerless.

I loved Wynell more for telling me what she felt through that book. We could speak plainly in ways that would never have worked on the outs. I was humbled that her faith in words, in language, and in the courage of Angelou to "tell so much truth" allowed us to shorten the distance between the colors of our skin and to find refuge in our similarities, rather than in our differences. This bond we carved out of our differences was a radical opening.

That opening, pried ajar by Wynell sharing her book with me, led to new and painful insights into my own life, to see the situations when as a teacher I had sometimes been condescending—throwing around my liberalism without really comprehending their suffering—or those rare times when I'd generalize, or laugh at someone's racist joke just to be polite. That she trusted me and loved me allowed for a certain wisdom to peek around the darkness inside me. This wisdom had come at an enormous price. Propped open as such by being incarcerated with people of color, as a white woman, I had to look at things I once refused to see. And I wasn't too happy about the contents of my heart.

Maybe paying the price that I paid for my incarceration was a gift, not a penalty, for a new courage that was allowing me to turn within. I was a stubborn and unyielding person in my addiction. Jail might have been a lucky break given the alternative—death. Or worse. What if I had injured or killed someone driving drunk? I don't know what it was about Wynell reading to me, inviting me into her world, and trusting me with her rage and depression about the way white people treated her that opened me up to myself. A new knowledge took shape, a deeper peeling back of my complacency, ushered in on the spines of our books. I was floored again by the power books had to unite, to heal, and to reveal even the things that we don't want to see. It wasn't necessarily pleasant, the way I was beginning to feel, because it meant I had to acknowledge a certain level of ignorance, even as I had always considered myself tolerant and fair. It turned out I was being invited to go deeper, to understand more wisely the issues, the frustration, the anger that people of color experienced *every single day of their lives.* This was powerful. I felt myself changing as I began to see the things that would help me claim my authenticity as a human among humans. What amazed me, of course, and what I loved because I was a writer, was that these discoveries were, ironically, coming alive and finding their freedom by reading precious books behind a locked-down jail cell door.

One night, after Wynell and I exhausted recounting all the TV episodes we could, and read to each other till our eyes practically bled, she pulled out another small book.

"The pastor gave this to me."

It was Psalm 91, her favorite psalm. She asked me to write it down and to pray it for her forever. So I wrote it on the inside cover of *Unbroken*. I felt all right about learning to love this psalm because it came from the Torah, and so somehow it was kosher to me to love it. Like me, Wynell was rightfully suspicious of organized forms of religion, but this prayer was beautiful, and we both acknowledged it. Her faith in this prayer alone opened my eyes. I began to soften toward the old God that I believed had betrayed me and imagine, maybe just a little, something new. Maybe the God that I thought had left me was actually a God I had to get rid of. Maybe, just maybe, there was divine wisdom out there, and I needed to find it in a different way, with different eyes and deeper yearning.

Wynell's favorite part of the psalm was this:

> *You will not fear the terror of the night,*
> *nor the arrow that flies by day,*
> *nor the pestilence that stalks in the darkness,*
> *nor the plague that destroys at midday.*
> *A thousand may fall at your side,*
> *ten thousand at your right hand,*
> *but it will not come near you.*
> *You will only observe with your eyes*
> *and see the punishment of the wicked.*
>
> *If you say, "The Lord is my refuge,"*
> *and you make the Most High your dwelling,*

no harm will overtake you,
no disaster will come near your tent.

We spent a lot of time extracting meaning from the verses. It was like a mini Midrash study—which is the Hebrew word for seek or study; the process that Jews use when interpreting the Torah. But for Wynell it was the promise of peace in the home, that "no disaster will come near your tent," which enabled her to sleep at night. And it comforted me, too, because I had developed a near-panic fear that something would happen to my husband and daughter while I was locked up. That our house would burn down, that they would die in a car wreck. Often I would worry that Greg would get sick and there would be no one to take care of my daughter. So I took Wynell's advice to read it every day upon awakening, and I fell in love with the promise of safety the psalm evoked, even if I could not locate a narrative for a God in my life then.

That night after the deputy turned the lights down, Wynell and I were unable to sleep. In the sad, amber glow of our cell, I remember feeling stirred up, despite the fact that the jail seemed quieter than usual. It was into that tense, hushed place that Wynell began to tell her story, first softly, then in a torrent. Somehow this confession, as it were, was different than anything she'd told me before. It was without bravado, and carried the badge of truth and the profundity of lamentation. She wept but didn't make a sound, tears streaming down her cheeks. As with Duckie before her, it was a story about poverty, deprivation, sexual violence, police brutality, and fear, just like Angelou's story. I remained still and quiet. I didn't want to spoil her story with my words. I knew she just wanted to be listened to, like everyone does.

Afterward, she asked me if she could move her mattress to the floor next to me and sleep beside me that night. I thought of Melissa crawling in beside me that first night I was locked up in a cell.

"Yes," I said. "Here, take my extra blanket." I gave her the blanket that Duckie had given me.

We slept like that, not just that night, but almost every night afterward. We both had a bad case of the fears. We had both known spiritual drought and failure. We had both made hard work of sorrow. In each other, to our mutual surprise, we found solace and comfort.

CHAPTER FIVE

EBI Module: Dayroom

In the process of discovering bodhichitta, the journey goes
down, not up . . . It's as if the mountain pointed toward the
center of the earth instead of reaching into the sky. Instead of
transcending the suffering of all creatures, we move toward
the turbulence and doubt. We jump into it. We slide into it.
We tiptoe into it. We move toward it however we can.
—Pema Chödrön, *When Things Fall Apart*

Every act of resistance, however small, was a victory. Wynell
was a master at getting away with shit. In addition to the
"falls" she took from her upper bunk, which allowed her up to
eight hours in medical, a change of scenery, extra lunch, and
maybe some good meds, she took full advantage of the fact that
our sink broke and remained that way for days. She managed to
convince the deputy to leave our door open so she could refill her
water when it emptied. The bottle seemed to empty with astonishing swiftness.

"You're filling that an awful lot," the deputy screamed at her. She called him Bologna because once she'd seen him pick the rubberized, imitation bologna from a sandwich and throw it at an inmate in medical.

"Bladder infection," she said. You could get a male deputy to do anything for you if you used the words "blood," "vagina," "bladder," "ovaries," or anything else related to the female body.

Almost every time she went out there to fill up the bottle, she hung around and chatted with her "ho" friends in Dayroom who sat under the stairs laughing at everything. When the deputy would shout at her to get back to her cell, she would calmly finish filling her water—this would take surprisingly much *longer* than the drinking part—and then saunter majestically up the stairs, that crown I imagined on her head sparkling under the grim lights.

I didn't have the same courage. Or at least I thought I didn't until one day, during program, I saw the usual twenty or so inmates line up for Life Skills class. I'd been watching this lineup occur every day, wondering what the criteria was for the privilege of going to class. I was envious that they were allowed to leave the module for hours at a time. One of the students told me that on Fridays their teacher, Ms. Kiara (an aspiring comedian on the outs), let them watch movies.

When the deputy called out, "Life Skills, line up," she accidently popped our door and I was suddenly outside, walking down the stairs and into Dayroom where, without a thought, I lined up. I can't explain why I did it. It was almost as if I were being pulled into that line by an invisible hand. Somehow—perhaps legitimized by my association and friendship with Wynell—the trustees, who were all black and noticed that Wynell trusted me, were "distracted" as I slipped in while they checked people off. I remember one of them nodding at me to hurry up, keep my head down, just *go*.

My heart raced, but amazingly, I managed to slip in and landed a coveted spot in EBI. EBI stands for education-based incarceration, a strange and ironic name. Why wasn't it incarceration-based education? The answer to that is because *everything* in jail is such incredible bullshit. You could never look around Lynwood and say with a straight face that it was an education-based facility. I would guess less than 1 percent of inmates were getting an education there.

The parameters for enrolling in EBI were that you had to have at least six months left to serve, you had not earned a high school diploma, and you had a felony and were thus going to prison. So I did not qualify in any way with twenty days left to serve; misdemeanors, *not* felonies; and a graduate degree. Once in the classroom, Ms. Kiara told those whose names she hadn't called from the official roll sheet to sign a piece of paper and she would officially add us to the class. I couldn't believe it: I was miraculously a member of EBI Life Skills class. Over the next few days, though, I came to see that this time away from the module was a draw. As with church, I wasn't sure which was worse, being locked up all day long, or sitting around talking about the ways people expressed their anger.

In Life Skills, we did "thinking reports" every day. These were supposed to help us deal with our anger. The thinking report contained four categories that you filled out with the two-inch golf pencil they gave you: Situation, Thoughts, Feelings, and Attitudes & Beliefs. In order to make it even semi-effective, Ms. Kiara had to add two categories: Old Behavior and New Behavior. It seemed like the purpose of the thinking report was to show us how to manage our anger and our problems, but it lacked a crucial part of any problem-solving process—finding a solution. The fact that the handout ignored this was typical of just about everything in jail.

One day, a new student offered to share her thinking report with the class. Linda was a large black woman with a handsome freckled face and a deep and melodious voice. She read off her entries while Ms. Kiara wrote them on the board. Because they were hilarious, I kept all of the thinking reports we did together in class and brought them home.

Thinking Report

Name: Linda

Situation: My bunkie stinks.

Thoughts:

1. What the fuck is that smell?

2. How is she fucking men and they didn't smell her?

3. How is she taking a shower and she still smells?

Positive Thoughts:

1. Maybe she don't know.

2. Maybe she sick or has an infection in her vajayjay.

3. She might be kicking.

Feelings:

1. Disgusted, angry, puzzled, overwhelmed, curious,
   pity (I want to cut that bitch—is that a feeling?)

Old Behaviors: Ignore her. Be rude to her. Clean the
room when she gone. Find any way to get out of my
cell. Talk about her to my homegirls.

Attitudes & Beliefs: Bitches who stink are dirty. She
lazy with her hygiene. She slow.

New Behavior: Talk to a deputy.

This went on for an hour, then further devolved into a half-hour discussion of how to clean your vagina.

"Don't douche," Ms. Kiara said, pronouncing it "dowsh."

We were told not to use products like Summer's Eve, not to use sprays or soaps. I concurred. The cooch knows how to take care of itself, even though Procter & Gamble would have you believe otherwise.

Between EBI *and* church, I now had a lot of time out of lockdown. The Protestants, of the Pentecostal variety, did church two times a week, and I also went to Catholic services after the Protestant one on Sundays. Once I went to the Christian Science services, but I had to draw the line somewhere. In the parlance of jail, that was "wack." There were no services for Jews. And I didn't mention that I was a Jew, because the church ladies were punitive. Maybe like the rabbi who had taken the kosher meal from a Christian inmate, the Christian pastors would take away my seat in their services.

All totaled, when the "po-lice" didn't withhold program, I was able to get out of my cell for five or six hours a day. With Wynell and me telling jokes, reading books, and sharing our lives when we were stuck in our cell, time began to move faster and I started to feel better by increments. I started doing yoga in the "yard," an eight-hundred-square-foot patio that shared a wall with the 105 Freeway. This wall was two stories high, topped by razor wire and an opening through which you could occasionally see a bird fly by. The sound of the freeway was thunderous; the smell of exhaust overpowering. But I made sure to get out there every day after my shower and walk around and around and around, or practice yoga.

I had only recently returned to yoga, motivated mostly by the pain in my body that likely came from the "physical exertion" of my last arrest. I wasn't sure how much a man stepping on my back had to do with it, but I experienced back spasms on a daily basis. Instead of looking at yoga as an extreme sport, the way they do in Los Angeles, I began to try to understand how it could change my posture, lengthen my spine, and calm my nerves. I became interested in how to breathe with every asana, trying to determine at what point you breathed in and when you breathed out. I knew it made a difference. After my return from rehab and before Lynwood, I still thought I had to compete with the twenty-year-olds in an LA yoga class. I was usually the oldest person in there and no one talked to me, because once you turn fifty, you're invisible. I tried handstands and arm balances to show off, probably ruining my back even more. At Lynwood, though, I came to yoga for the first time in my life simply to heal my body. Once the stratospheric depression in lockup began to come back down to an earthly tolerance, I did jail yoga to breathe and to ease my physical maladies: creaky joints, hamstring pain, shooting nerve pain.

To my joy, a few days into Exit Dorm, the next three books arrived, and with them, the feeling that since my relapse I'd finally, indisputably, found my way back home to literature. I had made it through the first three weeks of my sentence, and looking back, I saw that reading had been arduous, that my brain had been pickled and was not used to words. Now, it seemed easier, less encumbered by fear and the illness of early sobriety.

The next three books were *When Things Fall Apart* by Buddhist nun Pema Chödrön; *Beautiful Ruins*, a novel by Jess Walter, a writing instructor I knew from my MFA program; and *My Life as a Foreign Country* by Brian Turner. When Wynell saw them, she laughed at me again.

"Mmm, mmm, mmm, mmm, mmm," she said. I picked up *When Things Fall Apart* and looked at the back cover. She saw the title and said, "Little too late for that, eh?"

"Fuck off."

"Maybe it should be 'When Things *Fell* Apart.'"

One day, when I was sitting around reading *Beautiful Ruins*, they called my name: "Schwartz, 531." I looked at Wynell. Whenever they called my name, number, or combination of the two, I always believed I was being released.

"Roll it up," the deputy screamed.

Wynell smiled. "Maybe you're out."

But my hopes were dashed within a second of leaving the cell. Outside, I noticed all the others from my Life Skills class doing that slow, defiant jail walk, their roll-ups in one hand, their jail-issued yellow duffel bags in another. Standing around, standing around, standing around, doing what we always did in jail, waiting around, then lining up, marching, lining up, standing, marching, waiting . . . again. We were being moved.

Once again, I was not the one who would be left behind. But I despaired of leaving Wynell. I despaired of moving again. I felt the pain of it in my chest and stomach, a tightening. A loud hum began to sound between my ears. And what would happen, I thought, if they learned I wasn't really qualified for EBI? Would they extend my time to punish me? Would there be other consequences? And who would I bunk with? I saw two women I knew best from Life Skills class, Rose and Tiffany. Rose was a gorgeous

Latina. She was very nice to everyone, mannerly and gentle and always smiling. Now she seemed agitated. I had never seen her like that before.

"This is bullshit," Rose said. "I'm sick-ass of moving around this shit fuck fucking shithole. God damn."

Beverly Hills Tiffany, with her yoga butt, Jackie O hairdo, and rich parents—she was in on DUI, but had previously served time in Florida for felony breaking and entering—said, "It's so fucked. So fucking fucked."

We all laughed.

"Hurry up, ladies. Let's go. Put your personals out for bag check. Hurry up."

I looked up at the cell. Wynell was watching. She waved down forlornly. I looked at my feet. When I looked back up, she had gone inside.

After a while of milling around, Wynell came downstairs. "You forgot this," she said. She handed me my "razor," which was jail-issued from commissary. Like most commissary hygiene products, it didn't work and I had left it behind. She also handed me a few apples and her bran flakes. She knew I was constantly, chronically, painfully constipated from the copious amounts of lard in the food. I was touched by this gesture.

"Wynell," I said. I wanted to cry, but I couldn't.

"See you around," she said.

We didn't hug. There was so much chaos. She looked at me for a long time. I felt like, in some ways, I'd never had a closer

133

friend in my life. We nodded our heads at each other. A tear fell down her cheek. I turned away first, because it hurt so much. The place was filled with women in various states of dress. Deputies screaming, "Hey, no shower shoes. Tuck in your shirt. Keep your mouths shut. Line up."

Duckie was there. She nodded, smiled.

"Hey, sister," she said.

"You coming?"

She shook her head. "Nope."

Then she covered her hands with her mouth.

"Oh shit," she said.

She tried to hide behind me, which was ridiculous since my entire body was the size of her left leg. She pointed at Rose and whispered, "I stabbed that girl's dad on the streets."

I glanced up at our cell. For the first time since our water faucet broke, Wynell closed the door on her own accord. When you close the door, it locks automatically. She was putting herself back into that cage willingly. I experienced pain so acutely that I felt dizzy, like I needed to sit down. And, as was my usual response to every adverse moment in my life, I felt myself gearing up for a fight, fighting against all the fucking bullshit of that place.

I fought *hard* every day to stay clean—there were so many drugs all around me all the time. I battled against time: stopped time, time vanishing, time passing me by. All day long, I shoved down the urge to tell the deputies to go fuck themselves. The painbody roared ceaselessly. Monochrome loneliness. And every moment of every day, I waged war against the enemy of all thoughts: that I got a raw deal, that I didn't deserve this *shit.*

My head was pounding. The grief, the loss, the fear, the loneliness just broke me open. And then, something happened. My body softened. The rigidity and dryness of my spine abated. My heart crashed open, reaching, not grasping but yearning, rising; my thoughts emptied out and I was still. The screaming, the chaos, the searching of my personal property, the haze of lights, the blue-clad bodies moving around, all of it stopped. Everything, silence. And I felt myself leaning in, like you would cradle a child, to all the hurt, all the regret, the shame, the emptiness, and the fear, leaning into the sight of Wynell folding, giving up, incarcerating herself. Leaning into the whole of my astonishing life. I yielded. I surrendered.

I knew that from then on, I could never be hurt again, that I would let go of my clutching for hope. I would release my grip on pain and avoid attaching to the thoughts that seemed to lord over me and determine every action I took, every emotion I felt. I had surrendered. Fully and completely. All this time, I had believed that if I let go of the fight, *they* would win. But my entire life, I had been wrong. Surrender was the only win. I felt my power surging inside me. I understood that with surrender came the one single truth: *They* no longer had any power over me. I was free. It was my most radical act of resistance. And it would permanently and irrevocably change my life.

I hadn't begun to read Pema Chödrön's *When Things Fall Apart*, partly because Wynell never let up on the joke. But I put *Beautiful Ruins* down and picked up Pema as I sat on the hard concrete ground waiting for the police to decide how to dispatch us. And, just like every book that I had chosen for my incarceration, this book was material to exactly what I was experiencing right at the moment I needed it.

> *Reaching our limit is not some kind of punishment. It's actually a sign of health that, when we meet the place where we are about to die, we feel fear and trembling . . . we don't become undone by fear and trembling, but we take it as a message that it's time to stop struggling and look directly at what's threatening us.*

I had to laugh. In fact, I laughed out loud, surprising myself.

"Why you laughing, *güera*?" an inmate holding court with her homegirls asked.

I didn't say anything. But I knew this: we are born with our fists closed; we die with our hands open. I had died to myself, alone, but also under the eyes of something ferocious and divine.

"Here," she said, handing me some personal pictures that I hadn't asked to see. "This is my husband. He's doing twenty-five to life. These are my kids. They're with their *abuela*. I miss my babies."

I looked at the pictures. The other women were gathered

around, including Rose, who would abruptly stand up, wander around, then sit down again, repeatedly, like a tic. What was wrong with her? She was normally so calm and settled. Everyone else had that glazed look I was so familiar with by then.

"Wow," I said. "Nice."

The woman with the picture nodded and appraised me. She winked at me.

I went back to Pema and sunk back into the sense that the books I had chosen were stalking me. They seemed to have legs and volition. Later, when I was home and I told Greg how strange it was that every book seemed to divinely refer to my experiences in lockup, he said, "You chose them. You must have known something."

I did choose them, but there was no intended design on my part. I didn't know, for instance, that I would need Pema when she came. That was the strange part of it. I chose them because they were books I had wanted to read, or reread, and I had not been able to find the time to do it in my regular life. I chose them because I was terrified of time and boredom. But the books had ESP. Not me. They arrived the way the people did: Melissa, Duckie, Wynell—to soften the hell. As if they *knew*.

Pema writes:

> *The spiritual journey involves going beyond hope and*
> *fear, stepping into unknown territory, continually mov-*
> *ing forward. The most important aspect of being on the*

spiritual path may be to just keep moving. Usually,
when we reach our limit, we . . . freeze in terror. Our
bodies freeze and so do our minds.

But I had not frozen. All the layers of who I once was were being stripped away. Every couple weeks I would die to myself and then come back a different person. I used the words "always" and "never" less. I began to stop hating myself. I even began to think that I had no "self," that I was just living every day in the moment I was given, without judgment, neither hating it nor loving it. I didn't think less of myself, but I began to think of myself less often. Some days, I clearly understood how I had blown it, but I also thought maybe that relapse was strategically, divinely created for some express purpose that had yet to be revealed. I began to realize that it didn't matter that I was incarcerated—I *had* broken the law, and if they felt I needed to be punished, then so be it. In a way, that wasn't the most important epiphany of the moment. What I felt in my bones was this: I truly didn't care what anyone thought of me. If people wanted to judge me, I was fine being judged. That was a freedom I never thought I'd experience. I knew my own bravery, but I didn't need to prove it to anyone. My mettle became my joyful secret.

"Stand up," a deputy screamed. "Hurry up, ladies. We don't have all day."

As if we hadn't been sitting around *all day*. The woman beside me who had shown me the pictures of her man and her kids helped me up. Her name was 18th Street, for her gang affiliation.

"Okay, *güera*," she said to me, "let's pray for Dayroom."

∞

Pema Chödrön was born Deirdre Blomfield-Brown. She was the youngest of three kids, born into a Catholic family in New Jersey. She was well schooled—a very prestigious prep school in Connecticut and then, later, Sarah Lawrence College. She married a lawyer and had a daughter and a son. Her family moved to California and she went to UC Berkeley, graduating with a master's degree in education. She and her husband divorced. She remarried and moved with her new husband to New Mexico. There she taught school, as she had done in the Bay Area, and raised her children. One day she was sitting out back when her husband came home and told her he was having an affair and wanted a divorce. She writes:

> *I remember the sky and how huge it was. I remember the sound of the river and the steam rising up from my tea. There was no time, no thought, there was nothing— just the light and a profound, limitless stillness. Then I regrouped and picked up a stone and threw it at him.*

What's not to love about that? Later she pinned a sign up on her wall. It is one of my favorite bits of wisdom: "Only to the extent that we expose ourselves over and over to annihilation can that which is indestructible be found in us."

This resonated with me. It spoke to me of the horror and seeming endlessness of my addiction, the way I still had not stopped dying. I remembered one day, waking up in rehab and understanding that within me was a small flame, that last bit of wick that had not been extinguished by my addiction, though I had sorely tried to blow it out. I remembered thinking that that fragile light was where God resided.

I was growing stronger every day. I felt something shift in myself, and it was, ironically, in jail that I learned the difference between compliance and surrender. I did not "surrender" to my sentence, I complied. In the world of addiction, you tell an addict to do something but they rarely will, and they sure as hell don't surrender. The ego of the drunkard is way too big an asshole for that. But slowly, of my own volition, I began to raise the white flag to my addiction and to make peace with the damages the disease had caused. But there was a meaningful distinction to me between the idea that I had merely complied with orders regarding jail, and that I had surrendered to grace regarding my disease. And the one had nothing to do with the other.

I had found a solution that would safeguard me forever. That I was finally indestructible. Courage seemed to light from within. I didn't think I could be hurt again. And to this day, I can say that while I have suffered many disappointments and life events, even the death of loved ones, I don't feel hurt. I feel practical. This is life: hard, sad, disappointing at times, even as it is simultaneously sublime, gorgeous, and good.

I was assigned a bed in Dayroom. I couldn't believe my luck. In Dayroom, you weren't locked in a cell. Due to overcrowding, three-tiered bunks were lined along the perimeter of the room set aside for eating dinner and program. So you had the illusion of freedom and sometimes you could talk to other people while you sat on your chair in front of your bunk. You saw and heard things that you would normally be in the dark about. Dayroom versus a cell was like the difference between an aisle seat and the middle seat on a plane.

18th Street was assigned the bunk above me, so my luck came with a price. She was loud and obnoxious. I remember that at the one AA meeting I was allowed to attend—and only because Wynell used her sway with the trustees to let me out and go—18th Street talked all the way through. Her behavior with her homegirls was so unpleasant that one of the deputies closed the meeting down early. But later we found out that was just an excuse—the deputies had a birthday party they needed to get to. They wanted us locked down for their convenience.

18th Street carried around piles of shit. Bags and bags of litter and scrap. She had more dross than anyone I had ever seen: more clothes, blankets, toilet paper, spoons (we never got forks or knives, only plastic spoons), sanitary pads (no tampons in jail), pencils, commissary goods, hygiene, salt, coffee, tea, and cups all came with her.

"Hey, *flaca*, how much time you got?" she asked me.

"I have two weeks left."

"Why you here?"

"DUI, suspended license, battery of an officer."

She laughed. "What'd ya do, call him a meanie-pants?"

"Something like that."

It still made me rage, recalling this abuse of power. But in jail, I grasped a bigger truth, a more painful reality. Now I understood that much of the time, especially where addicts and the mentally ill and the poor are concerned, justice isn't justice, it's personal. This explained a lot about why 99 percent of the people inside are people of color. The realization sliced me open. Sometimes knowledge is like being carved in half.

Meth made its way into jail via two vaginal routes. The first route along the royal highway was by subterfuge and smuggling. An inmate, either processing through or returning from court for a hearing on their case—someone with very strong Kegel muscles—had to elude the deputies when asked to squat on the ground and cough while a flashlight was shone up her vagina and ass. In cases like this, the meth or heroin stayed inside the body and was tugged out later for use or sale. The second method for getting drugs into jail was by an inmate offering her vagina (or mouth) to a deputy in exchange for him bringing meth inside.

Rose had been acting so weird the day we moved because she

was high. She'd managed to get her hands on vagina meth, purchasing it from someone who'd fucked it in. She was flying.

Being in Dayroom, I was grateful for the incremental improvements: I could walk to the faucet and get hot water for coffee. I could sneak a phone call in. Or, when certain deputies were busy with a female inmate in the officers' toilet, I could grab a Diet Coke out of vending.

I slept on the bottom of my three-woman bunk. All day, all I seemed to hear was 18th Street rustling through her plastic bags. She was someone who liked to cook in jail. "Cooking" meant ordering things from commissary—salsa, tortillas, canned meats—and making burritos. Often it involved throwing a bunch of wet, gooey stuff into a plastic bag, shaking the bag up and, voilà, a meal! Once, 18th Street made banana crème pie this way and offered me a bite.

"Have some," she said.

"Umm." I couldn't imagine eating something that had been shaken up in a plastic bag, then rolled out on the tables we ate off of by hands probably infected with MRSA. But if I didn't . . . well . . . that would be rude.

"Mmm," I said. "Very good."

I gagged it down.

"Have some more."

"Thanks. I think I'll save it for later. Yum." I nodded my head, as if amazed at the culinary magic of jailhouse cooking.

Our three-tiered bunk was right next to the cell where Rose was locked up with a woman named LaRue. LaRue had had

ADHD and a loud voice. She had a temper, too, that would switch on and off. With Rose on crystal meth and LaRue without her ADHD medication, I felt like I was watching two cats with their tails cut off, in heat, in a cage.

LaRue, who was also a hard-core meth addict missing most of her teeth, had just been blazed by the Lord. Induced by the euphoria of the meth, Rose, normally an earthy Catholic type, had succumbed to LaRue's evangelizing. For the three days she was high, she was born again.

I liked Rose. I didn't fault an addict like her for seizing the opportunity to get high in jail. If I hadn't been struck clean and sober myself, I would have traded all my commissary fireballs and Keefe coffee for a few hits.

When she wasn't on meth, Rose was one of the cooler people I knew in jail. After I'd failed to take a shit for a week, she cheeked one of her prescribed laxatives and gave it to me at pill call. Laxatives were the crown jewel of jailhouse medication. And I could afford Rose some privileges, too. Just because you were in Dayroom didn't mean you could shower and go out on the patio whenever you wanted, so we were programmed, too. When it was our turn to program, we usually did it with bottom tier, where Rose was housed. So when program began, I would sit by the phone and give it to Rose when her cell was popped open so she wouldn't have to wait in line. She had a sick baby at home, and her man was locked up, too. She was stressed-out and needed that phone bad. Also, for being high on the world's most effective appetite suppressant, Rose seemed to have a huge appetite for bread. Since I didn't eat mine, whenever she asked, I slipped my daily allotment (six pieces) under the door of her cell. It was no skin off my back and it engendered an intimacy with her that I enjoyed.

Rose also came up with the idea of throwing the apple seeds from the soggy apples I was sure that the prison-industrial complex paid homeless people to exhume from dumpsters into a pill-call cup. She lined the pill-call cup with wet toilet paper that was really just one long roll of barely composted tree bark. This might explain why our asses burned like hell, but why the apple seeds sprouted.

Since her cell did not face east or west, she asked me if I could watch her sprouted apple trees. She wanted me to put them in the yard where I did yoga. I agreed, and watched as Rose's apple sprouts thrived out there in the exhaust and tidbits of gloom straining through the mesh.

One day, a couple of women joined me in the yard, asking me to teach them some poses. Every day, my yoga "class" grew. As I helped the out-of-shape ladies move into poses ("Don't strain, this isn't the WWE! Don't hold your breath! Listen to your body!" "Bitch, my body be screaming right now."), I would watch the apple sprouts and swear they were growing faster than my time locked up was passing.

The sprouts were the only living green things in the entire place. You couldn't count the turd-colored canned beans or even the mounds of rotted cabbage they served us at mealtime as alive or even green. So I fell in love with the apple sprouts the way one might with a newborn. I often found myself staring at them, thinking of my garden at home, the hibiscus tree with its large magenta blooms hanging over the meditation area, the fountain trickling, and the snow-capped San Gabriels looming on the horizon. I would only allow myself to think of these things for the five or six seconds it took for all thoughts of home to break my fucking heart.

LaRue and Rose's affair with the Lord lasted exactly as long as Rose stayed high, approximately three days. When the kick hit, the shit hit. From then on, Rose did anything she could to get out of that cell. Which is why one day, as I was sitting around in Dayroom, I noticed a river of water pouring out of their cell, followed by every variation of "you motherfucking cunt" out of LaRue's born-again mouth. Rose had clogged the toilet with her plastic meal bags and all that extra bread I'd been giving her. Now I understood her "appetite."

When the deputy saw what had happened, he ordered both of them to "clean that shit up, you fucking idiots," and then they were placed on twenty-four-hour lockdown in separate cells, which is exactly what Rose had hoped for—a chance to get away from nutjob LaRue and come down from the meth alone. By the time her detox ended a few days later, her apple tree sprouts were about two inches long, lush and beautiful and spring green. After her lockdown, she approached me during program.

"Do you have my trees?" she asked.

"Sure," I said, reaching for them under my bunk.

"Go get me that bitch's pill-call cups," she said, pointing to 18th Street's pile of crap.

Rose was looking hale again. She was so pretty, even her elaborate *La Virgen* and gang tattoos appeared delicate and lovely. She was one of the few inmates who really made the blues look good. Her green cat eyes were always accented by her jailhouse "fake-up" mascara—a mix of coffee grounds, baby powder, and commissary lotion. And she was smart. She didn't care much for politics, so she was friends with everyone equally.

I walked over to 18th Street and asked, "Can I have one of your Dixie cups?"

"Go 'head, *güera*." She winked, then nodded to her pile of shit on the middle bunk. It was an act of uncommon trust that 18th Street allowed me to riffle through her bags for her collection of pill cups.

I brought the cup to Rose. She filled it with toilet paper and poured in about a teaspoon of water. Then she gave me half her apple sprouts.

"Thanks for keeping my trees alive," she said, handing me the cup.

"Wow, thanks," I said. I couldn't believe she split her sprouts with me, but there they were in all their sapling gorgeousness. My love for them was immeasurable.

After four days, the "luxury" of Dayroom was stripped from me, when a mean, coldhearted dragon lady named Gutiérrez decided she didn't like that her inmates had been replaced by Exit Dorm inmates in Dayroom while she'd been away on vacation. So she spent her first day back on the job moving us around. It took hours for this process to unfold. I was sent back to a cell again. At first, the dragon lady put me in with a butch lesbian who played Hitler in an EBI Dorm play about Fascism, an ironic note since it would appear I was the only Jew in jail.

I moved my mattress, the one-inch-thick plastic mat, and my "bedding" into Hitler's cell and put my new apple sprouts on the shelf under the stainless-steel rectangle they called a mirror. I was not happy about moving in with Hitler. Though she had played the Fascist with much clowning hilarity and she was smart, I didn't trust her. She treated me like I was beneath her, which always cracked me up. I mean, we were *both* in jail. Also, I didn't like the way she lorded over her much younger girlfriend. The two of them would fool around with impunity, right in front of my yoga class. Every day. I was never sure why the lesbians never got in trouble. It was almost like the deputies turned a blind eye to the way they openly engaged in sex, while reprimanding others for stuff like dancing or laughing too loud. I didn't really care what Hitler and her girlfriend did, I just wished they didn't have to do it in front of us spastic blue-clad yogis sweating it out on the years-old, filthy, paper-thin yoga mats some soul had probably once managed to get permission to bring inside for the inmates.

After I secured my apple tree on the mirror ledge, I went out to retrieve the rest of my stuff—mainly my books and my "hygiene" (commissary-purchased lotion, baby oil, and shampoo, all pretty much perfumed water) when Beverly Hills Tiffany convinced Gutiérrez to move me in with her upstairs.

"Because we both like yoga," Tiffany told her, with her oblivious pertness.

The deputy rolled her eyes and said, "Go ahead."

I was surprised that Tiffany had made this arrangement, but I was glad. She was more of a known quantity to me than Hitler. I went back to get my stuff—my bedding and my beloved apple tree. But the apple sprouts were gone. Vanished.

"Hey, Hitler, where's my tree?"

"What tree?"

"The tree. The little sprouts? I put them on this shelf."

"Sprouts. What the hell are you talking about?"

"The plants in the Dixie cup?"

"There's no plants in no Dixie cups."

"But I . . ."

"Hurry up," the deputy shouted. "Come on get your shit and get moving or I'll change my mind. Hurry, upper tier, forty-six."

"My plants," I said.

Hitler shrugged. "No plants here."

"You fucking liar."

"Who you calling a liar?"

"You, you stupid bitch."

I was about to cry.

"Hey," the deputy shouted.

Beverly Hills Tiffany, with her perky Jackie Kennedy hairdo

and her yoga butt, said, "C'mon, Leslie, before she changes her mind. I don't want to have to bunk with fucking Twynika again."

I left Hitler's cell an emotional wreck. The whole move from Exit Dorm had been chaotic and depressing, and now this. I was distracted, upended. Maybe I had left my sprouts somewhere else. Maybe Hitler had stolen them. I didn't know. I only knew that I had loved and cared for my baby trees, and now the cupful of greens was gone. My heart broke.

In my new cell, I once again turned to Pema. She tells the story of a man who, before taking his formal vow of bodhisattva, contemplated what gift to give to his teacher. The giving of the gift is a focal point in the ceremony. Students are guided to give something that's precious, that seems impossible to let go.

"As soon as he thought of something, his attachment for it would become intense," Pema wrote.

Every time he thought about losing one of his treasured belongings, he'd practically collapse. Later, Pema mentioned the situation to a visiting teacher.

He said perhaps it was the opportunity for that man to develop compassion for himself and for all others caught in the misery of craving—for all others who just can't let go.

I didn't know how to do this. I was angry that Hitler had taken my apple saplings, yet I couldn't even be sure that she did.

I had loved my trees so profoundly, and sitting in my new cell, I had to ask myself why I was so attached to them. Was it because they were green, alive, because they struggled in that Dixie cup and the jail-issued toilet paper and yet, still, *they grew*? They were both a part of the world outside and my world inside, where I was surviving the odious hardship of county jail. The tree reminded me that I could survive anything, that life thrives even under duress. Now that it was gone, I suffered. I did not understand what Pema meant by cultivating compassion for myself in light of my attachment to the tree. Why? How would that help? I craved to have it back. I tried to grow my own apple tree but nothing took root. I was devastated.

One day our locks were clicked open on our cell doors. I heard them all pop like a machine gun, one by one throughout the lower tier, then upper tier. I assumed it was time for a class for some group of people, but then after a few minutes, I noticed the women in my area walking out of their cells, slowly, cautiously, as if going out for the first time after a nuclear holocaust. One by one, women timidly headed toward Dayroom, then the phones, then the showers. Soon, people were smiling. Happy. Was this program? Why so early in the day? Normally only one tier at a time programmed, but all of us were allowed out together. Usually the TVs were turned off, but now, they were all running.

What was going on? I had no idea. But I, too, left my cell and lined up for a shower.

There was a different deputy in charge, a friendly-looking man who didn't say much. When it became clear he had let us all out to program together, on his own volition, I was flabbergasted. It was unheard of. One hour went by, then another, and another. In my entire time there, I'd never seen anything like it. The inmates were unusually kind to each other, too, and quiet. The deputy's trust changed everyone's normally belligerent attitudes. He treated us with respect and never said a word. He just sat quietly, his face open and kind. It was the strangest thing I had seen, and I realized it was the first time I had witnessed an act of kindness by anyone in power in jail. His trust told every one of us we weren't the animals they believed us to be. In turn, we offered him our good humor and our respect.

But like anything that might be perceived as good in jail, it ended all too soon. A few hours in, a blond-haired three-striped sergeant and her lackeys showed up and told us to pack up. We in EBI Dorm were all being moved to the next dorm over. And the inmates in the next dorm over, which held the GED students, were being moved into our module. Obviously this was absurd and unnecessary. But it was how they kept us in a state of anxiety and fear. I'm sure if I Googled it, I'd find the manual on coercion and submission they used. Even idiots know that if you just keep people moving, you will mess with their minds.

"Don't freak out," she said. "Everyone will stay together. You will all keep your cellmates. Now get your items and be ready to move."

She dismissed our new deputy, and any benevolence we might have been deluded enough to believe would come from her ended abruptly. She began screaming and ordering us around. No one was moving fast enough. We were all slow and stupid. This was my fifth move in twenty-three days. I tried to be strong, but I was on edge. Even in jail you get attached to things: the view from your cell window, the placement of the cell itself on the tier, the way you can depend on when you will get your breakfast and lunch based on where you are in the dorm, when you will program, when you are likely to be released in the lineup for your commissary, and what time you will be popped for dinner. Moving disrupted these small things we grew to depend on, and the worst of that disruption was the delay of my books and my mail.

Tiffany and I watched for hours while they moved everyone out of EBI into the dorm across the hall, and the GED students from across the hall into our dorm. It was a meaningless and chaotic enterprise and made me think of the Nazis and their "orderly" disbursement of human cargo. As the hours wore on, though, it became clear that Tiffany and I had been left behind, along with about four other cells of two inmates apiece. They'd run out of cell space across the hall, we figured. No one explained any of this to us of course—withholding information was one of their clever tricks to keep us in line.

For the next several days, we were told we would be moved and to stay alert for our orders. In the meantime, I remained locked in the cell, unable to attend classes across the hall. Then one day, the ten of us who were left behind were popped out of our cells, told to line up, and escorted across the hall to the EBI Dorm. We were going to class. So I threw a bunch of candy in my blues pockets to help me through the next four hours, snuck a bottle of water in my tucked-in shirt, and headed across the hall.

Immediately, it was clear the new dorm was much stricter and, if possible, much more dreary. This new EBI regime ran on a high level of discipline that included seating charts and searches, and trustees (kapos) wandering around checking you. I wanted none of it. I was afraid, too, that they would figure out I was in EBI "illegally." So when they passed out official enrollment cards, telling us they were going to check to see if we all qualified, I tucked it into the pocket on my blues shirt instead of filling it out, opting to stay under the radar. I knew, though, that without official enrollment, my days in EBI were numbered.

That said, I was fairly certain that since, incredibly, the LA County jail system was not digitized, and most of the record-keeping was still on paper, they would have a hard time following up on most anything. With two weeks left to serve, I opted to stay as anonymous as possible. I wouldn't push to gain access to the classes across the hall, but I would still take a typing class and an early-morning biology class in my dorm. When the doors were popped for those classes, I would sneak out of my cell and go down a set of stairs, away from the check-off point where the kapos scanned your wristbands. I would find a seat behind a giant support beam where I could not be easily spotted and read from handouts describing things like the human skeletal system or the conversion of sugars and starches to energy—information I'd learned in seventh grade.

That day ended up being one of the most interesting days of my incarceration. I was assigned a seat with some of my former dorm inmates, Hitler included. I knew that she had been forced to move because she was in EBI, but that her girlfriend stayed behind because she was in GED. Over the days that they had been separated, I had watched while Hitler's girlfriend wept nonstop. She was inconsolable.

Served the bitches right, I thought, even though I still couldn't be sure whether Hitler stole my tree or not. In any case, we sat there while the EBI teacher droned on endlessly about something meaningless—how to balance a checkbook or some lame thing that no longer applied in the real world—and I shared my candy, and volunteered my test answers. At one point, Hitler asked me how her girlfriend was doing across the hall, where Tiffany and I still lived.

"She's been crying nonstop."

Hitler's face fell. "Really?"

"Yep." *You thief,* I thought.

"Is she . . . is she okay?"

I shrugged. "I don't know. I don't talk to her."

Hitler looked depressed. She put her head down on the table. Against my better judgment, my heart went out to her.

"I'll kite her a message if you want," I said

One of the trustees walked by. "Keep it down, ladies."

"Kapo," I muttered under my breath.

Hitler looked at me hopefully and with surprise said, "You'd do that?"

"Why not? Just write a note. I'll give it to her."

Hitler smiled prodigiously. She got busy writing a note. Then she folded it up and told me what cell her girlfriend was in. I put the note in my pocket.

"I'll be right back," Hitler said.

She disappeared up the stairs to her cell. A few minutes passed and she returned to our table. She sat down, and out of her front pocket, she pulled the Dixie cup, smashed, but with the tree alive and well.

"Here," she said. "Sorry."

I started to cry. "My tree."

Everyone looked at us. I began singing, "Reunited and it feels so good." And the other women started snapping their fingers and singing along, until we were told to shut up.

"Thanks," I said.

She nodded.

"I forgive you, bitch," I said.

She nodded and smiled. "Thanks."

Later that night, after I'd been marched back to the side of the floor where Tiffany and I (and Hitler's girlfriend) were housed, I waited for program. When upper tier was let out, I went downstairs and kited the love letter Hitler wrote to her girlfriend. I didn't read it, though part of me wanted to. I have not seen anyone happier in jail than that woman in that moment the letter landed. She pressed her lips against the glass on her locked cell door and kissed it, then mouthed the words, "Thank you, thank you, thank you."

I nodded and skirted away and out of the deputy's line of sight before my kiting landed me in the hole. I had my tree back, and my heart opened to Hitler and her place in the world. I thought it took moxie to admit, while incarcerated no less, that she was a liar and a bandit.

Two weeks later, on the day of my release, I would pack up my tree and walk out of jail with it. I consulted a botanist about how to transplant and care for it, determined to keep it alive. I lovingly transplanted the tender sapling outside in the shade, as instructed, but an unexpected, punishing rain unleashed one night and drowned it. The tree died. Perhaps an institutionalized sapling was just too fragile to make it on the outs.

I think again of the words of Pema:

> *The only reason that we don't open our hearts and minds to other people is that they trigger confusion in us that we don't feel brave enough or sane enough to deal with. To the degree that we look clearly and compassionately at ourselves, we feel confident and fearless about looking into someone else's eyes.*

I understood then what Pema meant about turning inwardly with kindness, creating compassion toward ourselves as a road toward understanding our attachments and the blame and hurt we carry when the things we love are taken or lost. If I could forgive myself first—for hurting my family and friends, for the risks I took that might have hurt or killed another person, for straying from my own holiness—then wasn't it easier to let go of all my cravings? My craving for material comforts, my craving for the ease of my suffering, my craving for love, for attention. My craving even for a tree that grew in jail. It made sense now that if I held myself with compassion for all my flawed humanness—including my attachment to things and ideas—then my heart would be open to forgiveness and compassion when others took from me those things that I loved the most.

With my tree safely back in my hands, I am ready to move on to the next book. The days are going fast now—I will be out in two weeks. A new calm has taken over, but it doesn't last. Though I have adjusted to jail, a new panic sets in. What if they forget me on my release date? What if they decide, because they can, to keep me longer? I try to stay in the moment, to relax, but some days I feel an irrational, suffocating fear that I will be locked up forever. And there it is, that word again. "Forever." "Always," "never," "everyone," "no one."

I close the cover of *When Things Fall Apart* and gently place the book in my duffel. I try not to hold my breath, because my breath tells me I am alive. I learn to move slowly, to pause before I speak, to offer my tenderness to those around me. It is not always received, but I don't give up. It is not always easy either, and sometimes I turn away and hold anger and rage inside me. In the panic that always follows my discomfort and my yearning, I do what Pema says. I lean into it. I live through it. I ask it, "What are you teaching me in this moment?"

CHAPTER SIX

EBI Module: Lockup

The work of preservation demands that the feelings playing about in one's guts not be turned into action. Just watch their passing like cherry blossoms.

—Maxine Hong Kingston, *The Woman Warrior*

Tiffany was one of the singularly most selfish (and stinky) women I had ever met. She came from privilege and had more money than I did, or ever did growing up, but we both shared the advantages of being born white. She relied on her parents shamelessly for money and shelter. She was four years older than Wynell, but infinitely less mature.

On the other hand, Tiffany made me laugh to hell and gone. She wasn't funny, exactly, but there was something about her that made me laugh the way I did with my friends in high school after we smoked bong hits. But that young woman never showered, and her hair began to hang in greasy rungs from her head.

She had read in *Yoga Times* or some goofy New Agey magazine that it was good to go greasy.

"I'm not going to wash it the entire time because that way, when I get out, it will be restored to its natural wonder," she would say. In return, I'd roll my eyes.

The one good thing about Tiffany was that she fancied herself a writer, so we wrote poems together. I relied on an idea that I'd used on the high school kids I taught in East Los Angeles on a fellowship one year, saying that we should each write a sentence on a page, folding it down so the other couldn't see it, over and over again until we had a poem that we would read out loud.

Another night, I suggested we write a sentence or phrase on ten torn pieces of paper, fold them up, and drop them into a cup. Then we would take turns pulling these rolled-up sentences out one at a time, and each craft a poem around the phrase. Tiffany came up with the weird phrase "Bitches rattle trust no man," but it inspired me to write a three-stanza poem about the women who had held me all the way to jail and would be there with open arms when I got out.

Brave hearts, tougher than
armies of men with guns.
Those bitches rattle and trust no man.
They rescued me from my
bitterest self, replaced salt with
fruit, blood with Band-Aids.
They lifted me from the grave.

In another poem, inspired by the phrase "Empty ifs and random buts," I wrote about a long-ago love, someone I had practically forgotten about who I'd met another lifetime ago while at a writer's residency in Wyoming. Jail was funny that way, the way it made you think of things you thought you'd forgotten.

> *The land spoke in hushed whispers.*
> *Wind blazed through the cottonwoods*
> *and the night spoke of empty ifs and random buts.*
> *We sat on torn bar stools at the Red Arrow*
> *peering down the road to Ulm*
> *while the trains blew past through Clearmont*
> *and in the morning we could not find the pennies*
> *crushed along that cold, long metal rail.*
>
> *I'd hoped to bring them back to California*
> *and hide them somewhere,*
> *away from the loneliness*
> *that drove me to sudden quiet love*
> *along that tender creek.*

The good times with Tiffany were few and far between, especially compared to my other bunkies. Tiffany loved herself. She loved her stylish haircut and her pretty, angular face—smattered with jail acne—and her amazing body. She would work out in the cell, sending a stink of body odor that took forever to dissipate.

The sight of the sweat pouring off her face made me gag. I put a stop to that.

"If you want to work out, do it out there," I said, pointing past our locked door.

And one day, when her vagina smell overwhelmed me, I said, "You need to take a damned shower. Every day. From now on." She did, but it didn't seem to matter, because amazingly even when she showered, she still smelled like underarms and pungent lady bits.

She was one of those young women who flirted with the deputies and made and used jailhouse fake-up. She obsessed about her boyfriends, telling me the same dreary stories about them over and over again, and the stories always included the money, the sex, the drugs.

Not surprisingly, she didn't like to do chores. I didn't know that the kapos made the inmates clean the showers, one cell of two inmates at a time. A few days after we'd moved, our turn was up. I didn't mind at all. In fact, I was grateful for the chance to get out of my cell and do something that would take up some time. I liked to work. I had been working since I was fifteen. I loved housekeeping. I loved gardening. I loved teaching. I loved work that required organization. So I was grateful for any chance to get myself out of my cell, even if it meant cleaning showers. As a reward for cleaning the showers, we also got to take an extra shower after we were done, which seemed like a gift.

But when Tiffany found out, she threw a fit.

"Are you serious? I have to clean the shower?"

At first I thought she was joking.

"Yes," said Miss Mouse, the trustee who'd chopped up her drug dealer. "Get to work."

"I'm not cleaning the fucking showers," she snarled.

"Yes. You are. They don't get clean by themselves," Miss Mouse said.

As they went back and forth, I was laughing to myself. I had not seen such petulance for years, not since I'd asked my preteen daughter to pick up her room. Tiffany was standing there, hands on hips, whiny voiced, in a fit of miff, spoiled rotten. After Miss Mouse scarily stared her down, Tiffany went to work on one set of showers, and I on the other. But it was clear Tiffany hadn't done much cleaning in her lifetime. She used the mops that were normally reserved for cleaning the floors on the tile walls, and the rags used to clean the toilet on the faucet fixtures. So Miss Mouse made her do it again.

The huffier Tiffany grew, the more mistakes she made, and the more mistakes she made, the more she had to do it over. I laughed hysterically at the show, like slapstick comedy unfolding on a stage. At one point, she was so crazed she stomped down the stairs, lost her footing, and wiped out. Not seriously, but enough to cause Miss Mouse to put her hands on her own hips and say, "Girl, you done lost your rabbit-ass mind. You keep that up, I'ma teach you what you don't know, you hear me?" This only made me laugh even harder as Tiffany's puffed-up angry face turned bright red. I could hear the inmates in Dayroom snickering. The entire episode was better than anything on TV.

Like me, Tiffany had a master's degree in something—I think it was geology—and she, too, was a reader. In one of those mystifying jail coincidences, she found a copy of *Beautiful Ruins* in the "library" of Exit Dorm. This was so strange to me. *Beautiful Ruins* was a bestseller for a minute but not *that* well known, and it was also on my own list. How weird that she would find such an obscure book on the shelves of Lynwood's "library." I wondered who had left it behind. I would guess a white woman, maybe someone like me or Tiffany. But in jail, it was impossible to stereotype. Everything I thought I knew about what and who people supposedly were was forever stripped from me. Another one of the greatest blessings in my life.

In time, I would read *Beautiful Ruins*. It, too, had an amazing cover, very similar to *All the Light We Cannot See*, and Tiffany and I would trade stories about what it might be like to live in the cliffs above the sea in Italy. We talked a lot about that book and read passages to each other that we liked. The writing was good. Funny and smart. The theme was a monument to love and love's disappointment. Definitely not my world: I have been lucky in love. One of the things I liked most about it was that the innkeeper of the only pension on the rocky island kept everyone loaded on wine and stories. It made me feel good that I could still enjoy vicarious drunkenness, that I didn't need to get loaded to appreciate why it works so well for regular people who can, from time to time, bliss out of reality with a little wine or, these days, marijuana.

✺

On March 21, I realize I have been clean for exactly six months. So I take my golf pencil, and on the slightly brown, recycled commissary paper that I paid four dollars for, I draw a circle and then draw a triangle in the circle. On the sides of the triangle I write the words "unity," "recovery," and "service." In the center I write "six months." I cut the circle out by making tiny holes around it with my pencil and ripping it carefully. (Later I will have it laminated and will carry it around with me in my wallet.)

"Look," I say to Tiffany. "This is my six-month chip."

"Congratulations. I'm about to be four months."

Yeah, yeah, yeah, it's always about you, I think.

I stand up and say, "Does anyone in this cell want to take a chip for six months of sobriety?"

I turn around and raise my hand, "I do," I say.

I turn back to the first side where I stood before. "Here you go."

I turn again, acting out both parts, and take the chip. "Thank you," I say.

Tiffany laughs. "You're a lunatic."

"Yes, I am," I say, happily.

I realize it's okay to be ridiculous sometimes.

The funniest part about this is that it's not until I collect all my medical reports that I see my sober date was actually September 23, not September 21. And even funnier is that, before I knew this, one day after I was home, I watched workers replace a cement panel in the sidewalk. After they left, I got a stick and wrote "9/21" into the still-wet cement. Every time I see it, which is every fucking day, I crack up that I memorialized the wrong clean-and-sober date. It doesn't matter, though. As the books I've read so far have taught me, it's pretty clear that every one of us has only one day to live at a time, and even that much is never certain.

The books continue to arrive, to my great surprise and pleasure. My next batch included *The Woman Warrior* by Maxine Hong Kingston. That I had never read that book startled me: Kingston and I were both from the Bay Area, and we had both attended UC Berkeley. *The Woman Warrior* was practically a manifesto at Berkeley, and I was an English/rhetoric major so I read almost every book in the canon of fiction and nonfiction. How did this one get by, especially since the Modern Language Association claims it as the most commonly taught text in modern university education? I think it was a little bit of guilt that gave me the impetus to add it to my list. I remember going to a show at the Autry Museum in Los Angeles on Chinese immigration in California and seeing a beautifully curated exhibit that included Maxine Hong Kingston's seminal work. I realized, because I had not read her book, that I had missed some of the value of the show. I suppose this was my reason for adding it to the list. Regret is always a great motivator.

The Woman Warrior is one of those books you really needed a good chair for, and endless cups of coffee or tea. And preferably, it would be raining outside and a fire would be crackling in the hearth. None of those things were currently available to me in my situation. For someone like me, where any noise, even soft music, was like an anvil in my brain, it was exceptionally hard to focus, once again reminding me that I used drugs and drank myself senseless because I was hypersensitive to just about fucking *everything*.

The Woman Warrior was not so much a revelation, though it was, as it was a triumph. To have finished a book as complex and meaningful, and understand it in that place, felt like victory. And it made me think about the self-esteem–building that reading provides. Not giving up on a difficult text, plowing through, dictionary in one hand, aspirin in the other, always filled me with the elation of triumph. As I had felt for Mary Oliver, Laura Hillenbrand, and Pema Chödrön when I finished their books, I experienced incredible love, maybe even devotion, for Maxine Hong Kingston.

There are two things I like about this book. The first is, quite simply, its absolute gorgeousness. Divided into five chapters, each story conveys the rich tradition of Chinese folktale, memoir, and fiction. Kingston appeared to be floating words effortlessly across the page, but she used words that caused me to pause. Sometimes it would take me half an hour to understand what she meant by certain turns of phrase. The book was a symphony, complex and difficult but beautiful. Kingston's book taught me more about my commitment as a writer than anyone ever had, including my teachers. As I read *The Woman Warrior* while confined behind bars, I made a vow to return to my writerly endeavors, in spite of the ever-present vexation of my failures, to attempt to claim beauty again through words.

But the second and most exciting aspect of Kingston's book was that it not only defies genre, it refuses genre. She blurs storylines. Overlapping narratives rely on fallible memory, fiction, and myth. Without going into too much MFA speak, what Kingston does is what every MFA teacher tells you not to do, which is to adhere to a different standard of truth than "reality" or "facts," neither of which are ever really verifiable anyway. Kingston seems to tell the reader, through the book, that the only way to be true to one's story is to invent and blur the lines of what "really" happened and what you imagined happened. Police do that all the time, too. My arrest reports are a clear indication of mysteriously shifting "facts."

But when Kingston does it, this complicated version of the truth becomes an offering of relief and forgiveness. My own life was a series of contradictions. I had published novels with big New York publishing houses. I had a fabulous New York agent, huge advances, a film adaptation, dozens of translations. I had a gorgeous daughter, an amazingly handsome husband, the world's most beautiful dog. A fine house on a hill, with breathtaking downtown and mountain views *that I bought with my own money*. I had friends who would die for me.

And yet I was a drug addict and a vodka-swilling drunk and now a jailbird. I broke laws. I broke treasured possessions during incomprehensible rages. I threw my wedding ketubah across the room, smashing the glass and the frame, and mowed down my husband's motorcycle. On purpose. I lost those friends who would die for me. I betrayed my family. I might as well have burned my money, given how I lost it to my addiction. I lived in a state of fury that had evolved over time—out of a childhood that baffled and wounded me, and later, in college, via an attack one night by a stranger in my house, a source of anxiety and trauma that held me hostage for two decades.

It is incomprehensible to me, and at the same time, it makes perfect sense why I fell so far. On the one hand, I was compelled by my addiction to not just blur, but obliterate the lines of my story. I was not an integrated human from out the gate. And what I came to understand, in fact the key to my recovery, was that as an alcoholic and a drug addict, I should expect no sympathy for this condition of mine. On the contrary, I learned that addicts like me should assume no such understanding, nor should we seek it. Long before brain and genetic discoveries had proven beyond doubt that our DNA can signal the likelihood of contracting diseases like cancer, addiction, and Alzheimer's, I knew intuitively that the science of alcoholism and addiction would never matter.

Such knowledge wouldn't help me find recovery, and it wouldn't help others find understanding or patience for those of us mired in the disease.

Why? Because my disease is spiritual in nature. Though I possess the genetics, there is no cure but one: finding a way to fill my God-sized hole. My mom told me I came out kicking and screaming. Looking back at my life, I never stopped kicking and screaming even when there was no visible target. My place in the world was always a place of warfare and antagonism. The more I drank and used drugs, the more bitter I grew and the uglier the world looked. Like in Kingston's "No Name Woman," the travesty of a life that defies integration is a story of screens and vapors, and ultimately incomprehensible demoralization. I was unable to accept life on its own terms. I couldn't live in, let alone see, the truth.

What those of us in recovery know is that few in society would be willing to believe we are sick, and even fewer would give a shit. Brain disorder or not, if we let it go long enough, addiction ultimately and often leads to criminal behavior, institutions, and death; all outcomes that inspire morality responses, not compassion or medical understanding, even, ironically, by most of those in the medical profession.

For Kingston the only way we don't lie in memoir is to create a different standard of the so-called truth. This is why the book caused such a stir when it was published, particularly among the rigid types who preferred that writing adhere to standard Western ideas about memory and truth, and linear timelines.

The Woman Warrior celebrates invention as a way to tell what "really" happened, and as a result, it resists categorization. Is it memoir? Is it a collection of short stories? Is it a collection of essays? Kingston seemed to be thrusting her middle finger into the contemporary literary ethos that likes its conditions about what truth is and isn't, and how stories should be told. She simply told her story the way she understood it, not the way people wanted her to, and it pushed the boundaries of containment as a result.

As I read it, surrounded by women—many of whom I considered warriors—I thought about how it is acutely and rigorously feminist to refuse categorization. I began to view the smart and fiercely independent women at Lynwood as too radical, too intelligent, too powerful for the mainstream. It would be ignorant to say that these women were here only because they were poor, uneducated women of color. Obviously that was a huge part of it. But in my opinion, they were also—at least among the women I fell in love with—way too smart for a world run by men, way too angry and defiant for the oppressive laws that men created, and not docile enough for a bully culture that enforces unjust laws.

I think about Wynell, and how she was incarcerated for how she earned her money, the act of prostitution. Wynell was crushed by the institutionalization of racism; her access to help was limited by poverty and bureaucratic red tape. She was destroyed by illness and a patriarchy that allows fathers to rape their daughters, and scares mothers into disbelief and denial. Her life is a reaction to her circumstances. Yet she is stronger than anyone I know. There has to come a time when we realize that the poor are powerful in ways the privileged will never be. They face hurdles and survive in ways people of privilege can't imagine. Wynell was in jail mostly because she was deemed "uncivilized" by the society that suppressed her.

And if hers were really a crime, the men who paid for her services, including the cop who paid her for a blowjob at least once a week while *in uniform*, would also be locked up with the same frequency and duration. But it's seldom the penises that go to jail in the prostitution scheme, only the vaginas and mouths. Who do you think made that up?

Before I went to county jail, I had been talking to that nun on the phone from the safety of my living room couch, the one who suggested I run for the bottom bunk. Somewhere in the middle of the conversation, she gave me a warning: "Be friendly but don't make friends. You don't sound like the kind of person who normally goes to jail. So you don't really want to get involved with *those* people."

A sick feeling washed over me when she said "those people."

I *was* "those people" now. What was she talking about? She also told me: "Don't share any personal goods. They'll take advantage of you." Duckie kept my commissary sign-on the entire time and *never once* did she steal from me. Wynell was so proud, she refused my offer for commissary, so I would write down all the commissary items she loved (but had no money to buy) and every week I would order them for her. I had to practically force her to accept those salt-and-vinegar chips she loved and the body lotion she needed. I understood how hard it was for her, how profoundly and deeply she could not accept gifts, especially from a white woman. I got it. But I still insisted.

I grew to pity that nun, especially for parroting the bully culture that lorded over her. How was it that she didn't think I was one of *them*? Then again, she was inculcated by a male-dominated culture, so I tried to cut her some slack. But given that she was wrong—pretty much about everything, including that I should selfishly deprive another person of comfort by racing for the bottom bunk—always made me think *she* should go to jail for the crime of being a compassionless bitch.

In *The Woman Warrior*, Kingston wrote that in an effort to make the Chinese care about each other outside the family, Chairman Mao urged people to pay respect to the spirits of brave soldiers and hard workers (not just ancestors) with origami replicas of houses and food.

She wrote: "My aunt remains forever hungry. Goods are not distributed evenly among the dead."

What I saw at Lynwood is that goods were not delivered evenly among the living either. Health care, jobs, and education were reserved for the wealthy and the white. Justice, too. There were countless rape victims among me, none of whom have found redress for the crimes against their bodies. For immigrants with fancy British accents (not Mexican or Arabic ones), American gates are open. The rest are forced behind walls or are relegated to their corners of the inner city to starve, to beg for help, to die of simple illnesses that just a little more money could cure.

But for Kingston it's the ghost of her aunt that holds power and sway over her. It's the scraping from below and the howling from the grave that teaches her, and all women who don't want to die with shame, to grasp our dignity while we are still breathing, to fight for our place in the world, to never *ever* give into the silence those in power want from us.

CHAPTER SEVEN

EBI Module: Lockup

*Ahead of them, a long way off, a range of hills stained by
mottlings of black forest flowed away in round white curves
against the sky. The lane passed into a pine-wood with boles
reddening in the afternoon sun and delicate blue shadows
on the snow. As they entered it the breeze fell and a warm
stillness seemed to drop from the branches with the dropping
needles. Here the snow was so pure that the tiny tracks of
wood-animals had left on it intricate lace-like patterns,
and the bluish cones caught in its surface stood out like
ornaments of bronze.*

— Edith Wharton, *Ethan Frome*

The deputies had their rules for jail and I had mine. My first
was never get used to anything about jail. Think of everything as savagery and obscenity. Take a shower every day no
matter how gross the showers are or how clean you think you
might be. Mop the cell floor, clean and sterilize the sink and

toilet daily. Call home every day. Yoga, every day. Never call your "cell" your "room." You have a room back home. It's got a fireplace and French doors with beveled glass looking out onto the garden you designed and planted. Your *room* has the bed you share with your beloved, and sometimes the kid and the dog. The family pictures adorn the walls, as does your wedding ketubah, repaired and rehung. *This cell is not your room.* Also, never raise your voice. Don't have fun. Never, ever, ever enjoy any part of incarceration.

The only rule I violated was the last one. I had fun with Wynell. She made me laugh. Her brain was searing, intellectual, and perceptive. We enjoyed many a scathing conversation about race, identity, our femaleness, our place in the world. With her, I felt ease and comfort. Anywhere that there is love, there is calm.

When I moved in with Tiffany, I can't say I had "fun," but for some reason, we laughed a lot. She wasn't very smart. She was too selfish for that, too self-absorbed. When you viewed the world entirely from the lens of self, you missed a lot of things. I can speak to that from personal experience.

As I rounded the corner on twelve days left to go, I had found women in EBI that I liked, so I had people to talk to during program. Denise, one of the trustees, was a favorite of mine. She had joined my yoga class because she was determined to get her blood pressure down so she could get out of her AB 109 jail status and transfer to the prison fire crew. She was in for insurance fraud and her circumstances vividly depressed her. In some ways, she was like me—she was a mom with a high school–age daughter, educated, with a good job. She might have received a tougher sentence because she was black, but I don't know. It was a first-time offense. According to her, she'd been an accessory, not one of the two key perpetrators. But one thing I noticed about Denise was she hadn't yet been able to surrender to the fact that *she broke the law.* It seemed like it was everyone else's fault that she did what she did. I didn't feel any antipathy for her. I understood; I had been there. She was kind, but she lived darkly under the weight of her crime. That kind of suffering was all too familiar.

It took effort and time to realize that the only way to move on was to admit my wrongs, make them right where I could, and live an honest, sober life. Jail got in the way of that for a long time. It is axiomatic that incarceration manufactures bitterness and shame. As I learned from Ruth Ozeki, bitterness and shame stand in the way of humility, acceptance, and transformation. Change is only possible through self-forgiveness. For me, an addict and a drunk, I had to remain emotionally and spiritually diligent. I knew I had to work harder than most people to live with integrity because my genes held the marker for alcoholism, and that biological microorganism was my kryptonite.

From a moral standpoint—meaning nurture rather than nature—my greatest defects of character were in the category of selfishness and fear. I was an utterly self-absorbed and frightened individual, but I wasn't mean. And I knew that sanity meant I had to stop blaming everyone for the fury of my addiction and its consequences.

I have no idea what a "criminal mind" is, but I know that I

don't have one of those. I haven't willfully hurt anyone. Once, when I was a kid, I stole a tin of cherry Sucrets and got caught. I loved those things. (When I told my husband about it, he laughed. "It wasn't even *candy*," he said.) Getting caught that day cured me of stealing. And later, when I was about ten, I told my dad that I wanted to rob a bank because "it was a victimless crime." He took pains to explain to me the costs of stealing, not just financially, but to my humanity and the natural state of its goodness. He likened it to the pebble you throw into the still lake. Every wrong choice sends out ever-widening ripples. I took his lessons to heart and lived my life accordingly. Until, that is, drugs and alcohol stripped me of my true self.

I admit that I take some comfort knowing I was being punished for breaking the law not while sober but under duress of blackout and addiction. But I also knew—admittedly this took me a while—that it didn't excuse me. Though I am 100 percent certain that had I stayed sober, none of this would have happened, the law is the law. I did break two laws. And our laws don't make room for mental illness. So I paid for my mistakes.

One day I looked out at Dayroom and saw a dog wandering around. It was the saddest dog I'd ever seen. Cowed, tail between its legs, it seemed to bear the weight of all the noise and chaos in jail. But unlike the human inmates, the dog had a lot of freedom to roam around. It was touched and hugged and allowed to stay out on the patio whenever it wanted to. I watched the dog for a couple of days from my teeny cell window, and in the evenings, I noticed a big, manly-looking two-striped sergeant taking it out then returning it again in the morning. Unlike most of us, the dog apparently had been sentenced to some kind of work-release program.

The next time I was freed from my cell, I made a beeline for it when we were popped for program. The dog was stationed next to a Dayroom bunk and a large, sullen Latina inmate.

"What's with the dog?" I asked her. She looked all of twenty, and she was clearly exhausted from being asked the same question over and over again.

"We have a program here where we adopt dogs from the pound. Usually they've been abused or something, and we train them."

"What happens to them after you train them?"

"They're adopted out to a home."

"Wow, that's cool."

She nodded, clearly bored. But then she said, "One time the deputy in charge of the program adopted one of the dogs."

I thought of that butch sergeant who I'd noticed taking the dog out every night. Early on, I'd seen her in Pregnant Dorm berate an inmate into tears, her macho, stentorian voice like a one-ton TNT bomb. The pregnant woman sobbed, holding her belly. The sergeant grabbed her by the arm and dragged her off somewhere.

"The sergeant who adopted the dog," I said. "Was it the big ugly one?"

"Yeah," the woman said, looking sadly at her own meager charge.

"Poor thing," I said of the dog that now had to live its life with a "po-lice" who thought nothing of humiliating a pregnant inmate in front of God and everyone.

"Exactly," the woman said.

The fear that they will not come for me on my release date, April 10, grows exponentially larger as each of the twelve days left falls away. This fear is like a vine overtaking the oak tree. I believe my thoughts. I live in fear.

I remember one day, while this meaty, red-faced Pentecostal minister went on and on and on about the fires of hell awaiting us when we die, I stood up. I couldn't take it. My body went into fear mode. Hell wasn't waiting for me. I was living in it every day. It felt like a buzz saw had gone off in my bloodstream. For whatever reason, I just *knew* they weren't going to let me out. It was irrational and unsubstantiated by all the evidence I'd seen so far where releases were concerned, but the certainty had become a full-body experience.

I saw Denise over by the vending machine, devoid now for weeks of my favorites: Milky Ways and Diet Cokes. She was talking quietly with Miss Brown. Miss Brown was in for dealing weed. She was hysterically funny. Somehow she managed to get her wig into the jail. It was black, with a red streak down the side. She *loved* that wig. She knew it made her beautiful. Whenever she walked to and fro, she patted it, petted it, brushed it, coiffed and fussed with it. That wig was everything to her.

Miss Brown lived in her own world, but she was never mean or hurtful. She had her own way that I found lovely. She would dance alone in a corner if they played music during class. And she talked like a southern belle. She was a lesbian and said she went down for her girlfriend, who was the dealer. She loved Jesus. But every time she went to the Protestant services, her face would reveal a world of hurt when the inevitable gay hatred rant would begin, as if she didn't remember it from the last time, and the time before that. She told me that she was gearing up for her transfer to prison. There was some story about how she was just going upstate for a psych eval, and that she'd be back or released. But it made no sense. They wouldn't send anyone upstate who hadn't been convicted. I knew she was not coming back to Lynwood.

Once in Life Skills class, she took the teacher to task for making a blanket statement about "you people." I can't recall the exact details, but I was amazed. She was fearless, empowered, and in the end, she was right. I remember being wholly impressed not just by her locution and the logic of her arguments, but her power and her fearlessness. I thought she would have made a great lawyer.

After the anxiety episode triggered by the hateful Protestant minister, I walked over to Denise and Miss Brown, knowing at some point I would be the target of the deputy's wrath for getting up and leaving church. I didn't care.

"I'm afraid they won't let me out," I said. Tears began to stream down my cheeks, silent, no-crying tears.

Miss Brown wasted no time. She took me in her arms and said, "Oh baby. Oh baby. Don't you worry about a thing. You gon' be all right. They don't got no right to keep you even one minute over your date. Don't you worry. I know you is feeling some type of way, but you got to trust God."

Her words calmed me. I was soothed by her certainty. I said, "Are you sure?"

"Oh yes, baby. Don't you worry. You'll be home in no time. They ain't got no right to keep you. You done your time. You go on and trust God."

I did not return to the service that day. Instead, I asked the deputy if I could sit on the back patio. I told her I was not feeling well. The deputy, to my surprise, said yes. I must have looked pretty bad. The dog was out there on a cozy bed. I noticed how nice and thick his mattress was. There was a bowl of food next to him. And toys. And lots of water. The dog was miserable, though. I snuggled up next to him.

"Hello, baby, baby, baby," I said.

He wagged his tail forlornly.

"You have a nicer bed than me," I said. "So that's good."

He looked at me with deep, searching eyes.

"And toys."

He put his head down on my leg.

"Don't worry," I said. "One day you will be free."

I sat quietly for another hour or two alone out there with the dog before finally I was marched back to my cell. Tiffany said something to the deputy that got me locked back up. Something like, "She's just faking it. She does it all the time."

"You're a bitch, Tiffany," I said. "Why can't you mind your own damned business?"

"I was just worried about you," she said.

"No you weren't."

Her accusation stung. I was not a histrionic in jail; I was a stoic. That day, though, I was hurting beyond my usual ability to assuage it.

The next day at program, I looked all over for Miss Brown. I saw some of her homegirls and approached them. One of the homegirls was holding a plastic bag that looked like it contained a nest or maybe some yarn. I couldn't tell.

"Where's Miss Brown?" I asked.

"She gone upstate this morning."

"Oh," I said. My heart fell.

Then I looked at the plastic bag the woman held and saw a red streak.

"What the hell?" I said.

"Oh, that's Miss Brown's wig. They wouldn't let her take it, so I bought it."

"What'd you pay for it?"

"Some stamps. And envelopes. That's all she got to take with her."

I walked away. I wondered how bad it was for Miss Brown. How naked she felt without her wig. How hard it was for her to give up that one piece of dignity. I wondered how long her wig would stay in that plastic bag, doing nothing for no one. It was one of the few times in jail that I cried.

I chose one Victorian novel and one post-Victorian novel to read in jail, because, for me, reading relics like these is like watching movies. They arrived in the same batch, at the end of my time there. The first, *A Tale of Two Cities*, I selected out of guilt. When I'd read it in high school, I found it so inscrutable that I never finished it and looked it up somewhere—they didn't have Google then but they had something like CliffsNotes—and bluffed my way through the paper I had to write. So I thought, in honor of my beloved AP English teacher Ms. Janowsky, I would finally read it.

I still found it inscrutable. And one more time, I never finished it. It didn't help that the book was some cheap-ass printing with no margins and a tiny font. The writing was so dense and, for me, unevocative (forgive me, Dickens) that I just decided I'd be cool with going to my grave not having ever read it. If I met Ms. Janowsky in the afterlife, I'm sure I'd hear all about it. I imagined our encounter in the clouds, Ms. Janowsky in her polyester slacks, her short hair, her big 1970s glasses. All we'd do is gab about books *for eternity*. Ah, heaven.

I also wanted to read *Ethan Frome*, as I was a huge fan of Edith Wharton. Wharton was nominated for the Pulitzer Prize three times and won in 1920, the first woman ever to win the honor, and one of only 47, compared to 825 men, who've won since the prize's inception. She was something of a literary hero to me, even though typically I was not a fan of the super-rich. She was a woman of means, who married well, but she had to fight tooth and claw to write and to educate herself. That her career thrived in the 1920s was a testament to her ability to rise above the confining social and cultural structures that caused most women to suffer back then.

Wharton attempted to write her first novel at age eleven. At fifteen, she published her first translation of a German poem. Unfortunately, since upper-class women's names were only published in relation to their engagements, their marriages, the birth of their children, and of course their deaths, she had to use a different name. The name she chose was a friend of her father's, E. A. Washburn. Washburn eventually became an ordained minister who wrote *Social Law of God* and was a cousin of Ralph Waldo Emerson. She did earn fifty bucks for the publication. I always wonder what she did with the money, which in 1885 was a princely sum. (About $1,200 today.)

In 1914, as World War I raged, Wharton opened a "workroom" for unemployed women in Paris, where the ladies were fed, clothed, and paid one franc a day. A fledgling sewing business of poor, destitute women began to thrive under her stewardship. After the Germans bombed Belgium, Wharton founded the Children of Flanders Rescue Committee and gave shelter and sanctuary to nine hundred refugees who fled their homes.

I had never read *Ethan Frome*. When it arrived, like *A Tale of Two Cities*, the poorly bound paperback was flimsy and the font size so minuscule I almost broke an eyeball reading it. But I loved the book. If you ever feel like crap about your own life, this is the book to read. *Everything* will look better afterward.

I did not read this book to analyze it. I read it for pure entertainment, the way people read *Fifty Shades of Grey* and the *Twilight* series. Here's the Hollywood synopsis version of the story: In the novel, the title character, Ethan Frome, is married to a woman named Zeena. He falls in love with Zeena's cousin, a young, penniless girl named Mattie. Zeena, who is always sick (read: bitter malingerer), brings Mattie into the house to live with them in exchange for doing the housework. One day, Zeena wakes up in one of her scary sick moods. She announces she is going overnight to a new doctor. She leaves Ethan and Mattie alone and the two lovebirds share a romantic dinner. But the cat breaks the pickle dish. I *love* this detail. Of all things, a *pickle dish*. Of course it was a wedding gift. (Wharton and novelists of that era in general weren't known for their subtlety.)

When Zeena returns home and finds the pickle dish in pieces, she convulses into a tantrum. Ethan explains that the pickle dish was broken by the cat, but Zeena doesn't believe it. She's no dummy. She's figured out that her husband has a thing for Mattie, so she announces that Mattie will be leaving the following day. At first, Ethan thinks he'll run away with Mattie. But then he chickens out, blaming money and guilt for not allowing him to follow his heart. As Ethan drives Mattie to the train, they decide to sled down the infamous hill where, at the bottom is the "death" tree, a giant elm that could kill the careless sledder. The idea is that since they can't have each other, they might as well kill themselves.

Mattie whispers hotly into Ethan's ear, "Right into the big elm. You said you could. So 't we'd never have to leave each other any more."

When I read this I thought of punk rocker Sid Vicious and his lover, Nancy Spungen, whose codependent relationship ended in her death and eventually his death by overdose in the claustrophobic Chelsea Hotel in New York City. I saw Mattie and Ethan as the 1920s New England equivalent—albeit without the vomiting, the heroin, and the knives. They had that desperate passion and the same kind of death wish. The "if I can't have you, I'll kill you" sort of thing.

Ethan responds to her idea with: "Why, what are you talking of? You're crazy!" He groans. The words are "like fragments torn from his heart." But she convinces him that if he doesn't do it, she will be destitute and alone. He insists that she sit behind him even if it means he won't be able to steer.

"Because I want to feel you holding me," he says, a little creepily.

They take off, faster and faster until they smash into the elm but then the unthinkable happens. They *don't die*. They would have been better off throwing themselves into an oncoming train. Mattie is permanently brain damaged, and Ethan has destroyed his spine. Zeena gets herself together enough to take on the lifelong task of caring for both of them. In punishing irony, Ethan's dream did come true—he spent the rest of his days with his forbidden love, but unfortunately she was crazy and his mean old wife was a constant presence between them.

The moral of the story: that's what you get for not following your heart.

Though Ethan and Mattie never consummated their love, I might argue that the whole sleigh ride thing was a giant metaphor for passionate sex. The language is feverish and lusty. "Her breath on his neck set him shuddering." "There was a sudden drop, then a rise, and after that another long delirious descent." "They were flying indeed, flying far up into the cloudy night."

As they near the final moment—that shattering orgasmic deathly moment—"her blood seemed to be in his veins." Finally, "There was a last instant when the air shot past him like millions of fiery wires; and then the elm . . ."

It seemed like "elm" was code for "orgasm," I remember thinking. But was I reading this like a sex scene—and a pretty spicy one at that—because I was locked up with a bunch of

vaginas and I hadn't had sex in weeks? How could the most depressing story in the entire world make me think of Greg? How
I missed him in that moment as those two crazy kids smashed
themselves so lovingly into a tree.

It was perhaps the perversion of being locked up that brought
on my desire to make love to my husband at that moment, but it
was no less a response that came from the true, subaqueous,
down-reaching love that Greg and I had for each other. I remembered the day we met. The story sounds like it could come
from the pages of a Victorian novel so I won't write it down. But
there were gazes across the room, the sense of light, the magnetic
drawing together. He was the nicest man I'd ever met. And he
stayed that way, throughout everything. He never left me, and
though in the deepest, darkest days of my addiction he had no
choice but to take our daughter and leave the house—an act of
courage that only broadened and deepened my respect for him—
he never, ever, ever left me.

Now I was stuck in a twenty-five-hundred-woman jail (about
a thousand over capacity) with a bunch of horny women. Het-
erosexual, gay, both, neither. Some women were sleeping with
the male deputies—I remember one inmate's blatant affair with
this bald, skinny, five-foot-nothing deputy. I remember he had
really small hands. Those two didn't even try to hide it when
they disappeared into the bathroom. Though this woman wasn't
in it for the drugs, either.

Sex really was everywhere. I remember one time in church,

two women started macking on each other. The minister practically hemorrhaged with shock. She started preaching, the way you've seen it on TV, about how gays were going to hell. The minister knew the verses by heart, and she started expulsing them, droplets of spit showering the front-row faithful. I could not stop laughing. It was one of the bravest acts of defiance I had ever seen.

But by the end, I wouldn't care if I never saw another vagina again. Or talked about vaginas. Or heard about vaginas. One thing jail taught me was the myriad names we have for our golden pearls.

Culo
Chuff
Flower
Pucha
Vajayjay
Cooch
V
Puss
Concha
Snatch
Gash
Mi culo

I remember one night at dinner, a random group of us had gathered at a table: LaRue; Miss Brown; Veronica ("*Mi culo* be lonely") Vegera; JaQuanda, whose thighs were bigger than my entire body; Straight Crazy Wanda and her lesbian bunkie, Carl (short for Carla); and two women from 18th Street gang, covered in tats of *La Virgen* and the names of their baby daddies, and their babies, and their other baby daddies, and their other babies. And their homies who were killed in the "war" and their *abuelas* who raised them, and maybe a teardrop, if they were old enough because that was so nineties.

Tiffany was saying, "I just discovered that Keefe coffee makes for a great foundation base!"

It was hot dog night. I don't eat pig, so I put mine up for grabs.

"Who wants this?"

Practically all of them dove on top of me. Everyone had to eat their feelings as much as possible, so primo handouts like meat were golden.

Carl won.

"Thanks," she said. Waving the hot dog I gave her around in the air, without its bun, she said, "One to eat, and one to feed my *snatch* with later."

Now, counting down for my release date . . . eight days, seven days, six, five . . . I was viewing Ethan and Mattie's suicide love pact as one of the most erotic sex scenes I'd ever read. Contorted, twisted jail. How I missed my husband. I would have given any-thing at that moment to touch his face. Or his hands. Greg has the most beautiful hands. I would have given anything to get out of a place where *every single woman of age* menstruated at the same time. Where vaginas were meal topics, and hot dogs sub-stitutes for vibrators.

"I miss Greg," I said to Tiffany.

This was a mistake. Because any time you said anything to Tiffany, it inevitably became about her. Within moments she was talking about her boyfriend in Texas who was going to send her money.

I picked the book back up and finished it as she blabbed on. One of my favorite quirks of the book was the copious number of ellipses Wharton used. There are fifty in the prologue (yes, I counted them, because in jail you count everything). At the end of Chapter 9, I counted forty-three of them. I can't be sure if these counts are accurate given that I didn't really trust my print-ing of the book, but the point is, there were *a lot* of ellipses.

What I love about ellipses is they indicate the thing that's been left out. In the story, the most important parts are left out, just like they were in Kingston's chapter "No Name Woman." We don't really know Zeena's story, and we don't really know Mattie's either. The only relevant points—and this was clearly intentional on Wharton's part—were how financially destitute most women were and how few opportunities, if any other than marriage, there were for women of their time.

The ellipses were a brilliant literary choice. At first, I had to ask why, if Wharton was such a true feminist and badass social activist, she would leave out pressing details about the women. But then, of course, this is the genius of Wharton, who wanted to draw attention to the fact that women's stories are *always* left out. Even in the end, we actually don't learn perhaps one of the most crucial details of the story. We learn about the sledding "accident" from Ruth, who is in the story from beginning to end. Ruth is a fairly reliable character. She was friends with Mattie and knew the story all too well. She explains what happened after Mattie was taken in.

> *They gave her things to quiet her, and she didn't know much till to'rd morning, then all of a sudden she woke up just like herself, and looked straight at me out of her big eyes and said . . .*

But we never find out what she said. I almost threw the book across the cell when I read that sentence. But again, it was a brilliant move. All we know is that Ruth was frightened by what Mattie said and wouldn't repeat it. And isn't this just the story of women's lives even now? So many scandalous, shameful, unmentionable secrets: the beatings, the rapes, the incest.

What did she say to Ruth? Sitting in my cell, I tried to imagine. Maybe she said she was pregnant. Or that they'd had sex. Maybe she told Ruth the truth—they'd flown into that elm tree on purpose. Or that she yearned for God, or that she wished she could work, or how she wanted to write a book before she died, or that she dreamed of living alone unencumbered by marriage, or together with a woman. Maybe that she thought she was beautiful.

In the end, Ruth says, "I don't see's there's much difference between the Fromes up at the farm and the Fromes down in the graveyard; 'cept that down there they're all quiet, and the women have got to hold their tongues."

What the heck? What in the world did Wharton mean by that? Did she mean that it's a shame that women always have to hold their tongues? Or did she mean thank God for the grave so women will finally keep their mouths shut? I think she meant that women's lives are so devalued—in jail, so overprosecuted; out there, so hobbled by isolation and dependency—that they have internalized their status in the world to the point of acting counter to their own best interests. Just like Mattie, who thought the best solution was to bash herself into a tree.

Zeena was bitter and jealous. The pool of dependency was shallow and the pickings slender. There weren't enough men to go around. But Wharton literally "crippled" Mattie, making her a raging bitch in illness and frustration. She seemed to be saying that in a world of oppression even the hopeful end up bitter when resources are scarce and a woman's worth is constantly belittled and scorned.

The secrets of chronic abuse, of chronic misogyny, of being chronically underpaid, of being chronically raped, sexualized, and brutalized—these secrets kill us. The shame blisters, flames, and burns. Sometimes the only way to deal with that—for some women at least, for the saddest ones like those who would vote against their own interests, for example—is to adopt the prevailing culture's abuse, and incarcerate their own self-worth and ram themselves into their own metaphorical elm tree on their way down the icy path.

The women in jail had their secrets. Wynell told me hers. So did Duckie. But one thing I celebrated was that few of the women there kept their mouths shut. Even if in a general way, across the board, Lynwood was a sad campus of self-loathing, I knew that there was also a vivid celebration of outrage, of joy, raunchy, muscular, and brave.

Many of the women were there behind their men. Domestic abuse, for instance. I saw one woman come in with the most hideous beat-up face, to the point that she would probably be blind in one eye for the rest of her life. Her man had beaten her up. She told me he'd gone to jail, too, but he was already out. They were charging her, not him, with domestic violence. I had met some women who said they were locked up for selling drugs for their men. And one woman had written a fake prescription so she and her man could get high on oxy. "I took the risk," she said. "I didn't want him to beat the shit out of me again."

My fellow inmates were not silent women. These were women who knew how to get what they wanted, even if it meant manipulating the system. Unlike Ethan Frome's women, with their secrets, those I met in jail were open books. After I was released, I often wished that there was some way to take the whole lot of us, educate us, gives us something to eat other than McDonald's, free us from the bondage of drugs and alcohol, provide us with jobs, and *then* see what would happen for women's rights on the outs.

What my eyes saw was a truth that people either don't want to believe or can't. The incarceration of women for crimes of necessity—whether it's stealing food for their babies or money for their addiction—is society's dirty little secret. I met one woman who was sentenced to six months for stealing two pounds of turkey meat for her kids. Appalling. But in American culture, it's just business as usual to keep women of color and the mentally ill (including addicts) from attaining their power by keeping them uneducated, underfed, and incarcerated.

The mainstream, regardless of party affiliation, is complicit. Incarcerating those with addictions and mental illness doesn't stop the cycle of addiction and criminal activity. Instead, incarceration perpetuates the revolving door of substance abuse and the crimes that accompany it. And it costs a lot of money; money that might be better spent on mental health solutions that will make a difference. But for some reason, the logic of this falls constantly, frustratingly on deaf ears. I can only speculate as to why.

In *Ethan Frome*, Wharton definitively shows us the entrapment of women in a world that belonged to men. Sometimes it's hard not to think that this paradigm still exists. The irony in choosing to name the book after the man in the story who consciously but unwittingly causes the problems is a scorching and unforgettable choice.

I want to write a different book for us someday. The one that shows the world how unfettered our minds and hearts are, the one that shows our brilliance and our capacity for intellectualism, invention, creativity. The one that shows the Wynells and the Duckies and the Miss Browns of the world as they really are: powerful, intelligent, loving, and creative. In my world, we would break them out of a system that, without conscience or consideration, entraps their best qualities so that they remain forever invisible, crippled, and despised.

CHAPTER EIGHT

EBI Module: Last Days

He soon acquired the forlorn look that one sees in vegetarians.
—Gabriel García Márquez, *One Hundred Years of Solitude*

One day, when I had only a little more than a week left, Rose saw me sitting alone.

"What's up?"

"Man, I am constipated."

"You and me both," she said. "I don't have any of those ex-lax left either, or I'd—"

"No, it's cool. You already helped out. I just want to get to the doctor."

You had to see a doctor to get the simplest things. Antacids and laxatives were coveted in jail.

"Well, what's stopping you?"

"I put in a request two weeks ago."

She clucked her tongue. "C'mon, girl, you will never see a doctor if you do it by the rules."

She brought me up to the deputy's desk. "This woman has waited"—she looked at me and I saw instantly where we were going—"how long, three weeks?"

"Four," I said.

"Four weeks to see a doctor."

He looked at us with the usual blank stare.

"How would you feel if your wife was sick and couldn't see a doctor?" Rose said. "How about your daughter? What the hell is wrong with you? Look at her. She's sick."

I did my best to look sick.

"Well, what are you waiting for?" Rose said. "C'mon, man. She's bleeding from her vagina. And it's *not* her period."

"I think my ovaries are pussing over," I said.

He looked like we'd struck him with a burning spear. He quickly got a pen and signed an order. We could barely contain ourselves as we walked away.

The next morning, I was popped from my cell at 7 a.m. and sent on my merry way to medical. As I left the dorm, one of the trustees said, "See you in about eight hours."

She wasn't joking. Medical was like an ironman competition: long, grueling, sweaty, crowded, painful. Also, like everything in jail, it was a place where time came to a grinding halt. After a half-hour march through a labyrinth of hallways and elevator rides to pick up other inmates in various states of illness, we were brought to Waiting, until we were called. I sat with the others and let that familiar insane feeling descend, the one where it seemed like no one really knew I was there (invisible), that no one would ever call my name or booking number (abandoned), that eventually I'd be like a post in the snow that disappears when the snow piles up over it (forgotten).

After about two hours, they called me and I walked around a corner where they took my blood pressure—85 over 50.

"Holy shit, am I dead?" I asked. "And gone to hell?"

Nothing. The cunty nurses and shithole doctors never speak to you except to abuse you. My blood pressure had always been low when I was clean and sober, but this was ridiculous. All I could think was that I was in a state of shock *still*. Maybe the machine was broken, which wouldn't surprise me.

After that, I sat for another hour and waited. Then at one point, I looked up and there was Wynell. She smiled slyly at me and waved as if us being there together was no surprise to her. Joy filled me. I waved back. She nodded and disappeared—limping, of course—into some other room.

After that hour evaporated—it was sort of like waiting for a banana peel to decompose—I was marched to the official waiting room. This was a small area with a TV and about forty other inmates sitting around in school desks and chairs. Lunches were brought in. I gave mine away, except for the apple and the cookies, which I ate slowly. For me, food was a challenge. It was shockingly repulsive. The "meat," which came only in the form of hot dogs and bologna, was inedible. Only once did I take a bite, and it tasted like an entire skunk had been thrown into a wood chipper and rolled into soy additives and textured vegetable protein. More like something you'd use to spackle a wall with than eat. There was no fresh food except apples, cabbage, and oranges and sometimes an ice-cold green banana that, if not eaten immediately, turned black within the hour. The apples were almost always soggy. One of the worst meals—the inmates called it Scary Yaki—was a bowl of something that looked like wet cat shit and smelled like underarms and penises. I never ate it. Wynell, who'd worked in the kitchen during a previous incarceration, told me that they kept the apples in the freezer, which explained why, by the time they defrosted, they were like bacterial soft rot. One of her jobs, which she ended up quitting, was cleaning out the dead rats behind the stoves, ovens, and freezers.

I sat down and prepared to wait for another ungodly stretch. I had no idea what time it was—I'd seen one clock, but it had stopped at 4:13. I guessed, since lunch had arrived, it was around 11 a.m. That meant I'd been sitting for four hours and done nothing much except find out that, according to my blood pressure, I was practically in a coma. Then the door opened and in sauntered the queen. She had that smile on her face—the one that told me she'd "fallen" again and was "badly injured."

"Wynell!" I said. I got up to hug her. I was way too uncool in my enthusiasm and joy. She never wanted anyone to see us demonstrating affection.

"What the fuck?" I said.

"Denise told KRS-One you were here. And KRS-One told me, '"Hey, girl, you're ex-bunkie is down in medical.' So . . ." She suddenly limped and then we both laughed.

KRS-One, as was Wynell's style, was the nickname she'd given a trustee who did bear a striking resemblance to the rapper of the same name. I was moved that Wynell faked an injury to spend time with me in medical. We had four hours together. It was one of the best days of my time there. She told me what had been happening next door in Exit Dorm. I asked her about her "ho" friend Princess, who'd one day been dragged over to our dorm and handcuffed to a chair outside.

"We had to go on lockdown because of that bitch," I said.

"Yeah, she stupid," Wynell said. "She got into it with Cookie."

She had a few days left. I had a few days and a week left.

"Promise me you'll call me when I get out," I said.

"April 10th. I remember. I promise."

When I was called in to see the doctor, I said, "Okay, then."

"Go on. I'm sure I'll still be here when you get back."

When I saw the doctor, time sped up. All those hours of waiting for what I remember as maybe three mostly abusive minutes with the doctor.

"Why are you constipated?" she asked with that accusatory tone I had become accustomed to by this point of my time served. As if it were my fault that all we ate was lard, hard-boiled eggs, and peanut butter. One thing I noticed: as they were abusing us with their accusations and insults, they did so as if we were forcing them to be assholes. Couldn't we see how exhausting it was for them to treat us like shit?

After a few more brusque questions, she said she'd get the prescription and that I should go to pill call that night and collect my laxative. I figured there would be a hitch—there always was—and that I'd end up getting my laxative on the day I left. Still, I was glad to hope, and I was happy I'd get to see Wynell on my way out. But when I returned to the waiting room, she was gone.

The following day, during program, Denise called me over.

"You teaching yoga today?"

"Yeah."

"Okay. There's a new girl here. Is it okay if she—"

"Of course."

As she spoke, she slipped me something. I didn't look to see what it was, but it felt like a card. If a trustee got caught kiting messages, it was far worse than if we did. I stuffed whatever it was in my gigantic pockets and gave her a hug.

"When are you starting class?" she asked.

"Five minutes."

By now, there were sometimes upward of twenty women torturing themselves into poses. It was quite a sight. Beautiful really. Women of all colors and shapes, grunting it out. One woman, a large gang girl with permanent eyebrows and lip liner, and her baby daddy's name tattooed on her chest, said, "Damn, why the fuck this be so damn hard? It ain't like we joggin' or some shit like that."

As I helped the squirming blue-clad yogis—I always asked first if I could touch them and no one ever said no—and threw in a couple of poses to stretch my perennial aching back, the kited message burned a hole in my pocket. When we were sent back to our cells and locked down, I opened the card.

It was a green Easter card with blushy pink hibiscus flowers on the cover. They looked exactly like the hibiscus that fluttered around the meditation corner in the back garden of my house.

I opened the card and recognized Wynell's neat, beautiful writing.

Dear Leslie,

Today is March 31st. I have one more day in here and you are right behind me. I pray all is well with you. I still pray for you. ☺ I miss the only other intelligent person in Lynwood. ☺

> *Praying for you as always—*
> *Wynell*

It was just like her not to use the word "love." She also enclosed a half sheet of paper, adorned with drawings of flowers and musical quotes, an elephant, a giant sun and hearts. It was titled: "Things to Try and Remember," and she listed all the hilarious things we laughed about and discussed. *Read Vagina Monologues—FUNNY SHIT! Watch Ashly Williams perform "I Will Always [Heart] You" on X-Factor. Purchase the book "Psalm*

207

91." This was followed by a drawing of a book with that title, a peace symbol, and the words "great psalm." The list went on.

She also included two Bible passages. The first was Psalm 4:8, "In peace I will both lie down and sleep; for you alone, O Lord, make me dwell in safety."

And John 14:27: "Peace I leave with you; my peace I give to you. Not as the world gives do I give to you. Let not your hearts be troubled, neither let them be afraid."

Wynell's heart was always unsettled by fear. That was why she loved any Bible verse, like her favorite, Psalm 91, that promised safety. I remembered how she would stand at the door every day and stretch and say, "I am at peace because I choose to be at peace."

For all of Wynell's bluster and bravado, she yearned for peace and safety. It was all she ever wanted, but it was the one thing that always eluded her. She would, at the time of this writing, be back inside Lynwood two more times, for four to six weeks each. And I guessed, unless something gave, her life would continue like that. All that talent, all that intelligence, all that beauty. Wasted by incest, denial, drugs and alcohol, and violence, diminished by secrets and the shame that kept them burning.

❧

It's probably true that most avid readers have read *One Hundred Years of Solitude*. It's probably also true that it's on most college and university reading lists, that a lot of people don't like it, that a lot of other people would make love to it if they could, and that, as an example of "magical realism," it's probably one of the most imitated and discussed books in fiction. I wasn't sure that I could add anything new to the dialogue about this book, and about its creator, so I almost chose to leave it out of this account. But then I thought, why not try to write a synopsis of the story. It was that frustrating endeavor that led me to see that, one more time, I was dealing with—and had chosen without thinking about it—a nonlinear story, one about time, memory, and forgetting.

If every great book is both public and personal, I began to realize during my second reading of *One Hundred Years of Solitude*, locked up behind bars, that the personal had become universal once again. Even in *Ethan Frome*, a book that in tone, content, and meaning couldn't be further from Márquez's masterpiece, Wharton chose to tell the story in both present time and flashback. It became ever more apparent as my time doing time went on and neared its end that the now is always too weak a space to hold all of our joy and all of our losses. The past is there, always informing the present, the future, and indeed itself.

Nonlinear structure might appeal to me because as an addict and a drunk, nothing in my life seems to have forward momentum. Even as a kid, being raised in a wildly capricious alcoholic home meant time and momentum, memory and history were excessively warped. Truth could never be understood, because the story was always changing, and it went back to generations of family members ruined by addiction. Both my father and mother were impacted by the mental illness, cruelty, and alcoholism of their elders. The endowment of suffering and confusion was a caustic influence on the way I experienced my world and the world around me. I was not someone who touched people, because we never touched each other in my family. Reality was contorted—other people's parents didn't yell when they were mad. Other people's parents weren't drunk day and night. In my growing-up years, hurtful words were normal. And as I grew older and began to have boyfriends, I chose people just like my parents and like me. Feral and childish. Selfish. Greg was such a nice man—the absolute opposite of my previous boyfriends—but still it took me a long time after we became a couple to realize that you didn't call people names when you were mad at them. You didn't yell. I'm embarrassed to admit this was a complete surprise to me. It was as if other people who were calm and kind were the weirdos, not me. But you only know what you know, until, if you're lucky enough, you unlearn the old ways and learn the new ones.

But it is also safe to say that such an unhinged upbringing influenced me to respond to my life in creative and unusual ways, collecting and organizing magic to mitigate a puzzling world. The intervals of love and rage were how I told time, but they influenced how I spent it, too.

My addiction story, my recovery story, my relapse, and my return can only be told in parts, looking back and then forward, then in the space between. Each relapse, each drink, each moment of checking out is only informed by history. Recovery's story depends on the past. Understanding it requires the future. I can't locate myself in so many of the narratives of my life, not only because that batshit-crazy woman isn't me, but because I have no memory of the events. Nor, for many years, could I acquire any sort of perspective or extract meaning even after I capitulated to the truth: that I would not be free until I learned the details of what happened. I remember telling a friend that I was investigating my own 414-day blackout and she said, quite plainly, "Are you crazy?"

Yes, and no. I felt crazy not knowing what happened, and I acted crazy during the two years it took to collect the data and hear the stories. I don't feel crazy now. But then, I walked around in a low-level depression, aghast at the power of my addiction to destroy everything in its path. I saw the addiction as something separate from me, or rather like the alien that took over Sigourney Weaver's body. A fungus growing monstrous the more I fed it. All I knew to be true before I started was that after 414 days of blackout, I woke up one day in a rehab in Santa Fe, New Mexico, with the impression of an LAPD cop's boot clearly visible on my back. What I discovered when I was done with my investigation was that truth is malleable in the retelling and that in the end I had hurt a lot of people. The details mattered to them. Amends were compulsory.

I might be able to conclude that my passion for nonlinear

storytelling is about knowing, as Ozeki showed me, that time in its clock-on-a-wall form, and story as linear, like a yardstick, is often the least truthful way to talk about or understand its passage. All stories can only be re-created by collapsing the past, the present, and the future. We are not what we do, like a résumé. Jail, for all its insidious horror, its odious dehumanization, its dependence on the momentum of days, of counting along the agonizing progress of calendars facing ever forward, is really a place that embraces no time, for which there is no clear understanding of its movement. In jail, time moves backward and forward. It is without symmetry, a starfish with five arms and no central brain. We are not, it turns out, simply our crimes or our release dates. We are where we came from. We are how we change. We are what we remember, and what we don't remember. We are the moments that pass, and also the moments that stand still. Time is not our enemy but our puppet. Memory is prophecy and what we think is real is just an illusion.

My husband called my relapse the Great Unpleasantness. Years later, we no longer live daily in the realm of that era, but my family conducts itself every day as if informed by its message. For a long time afterward, we tiptoed through the days, memory at our backs. For them, the memories were all too real. For me, having little to no recollection of what transpired over those 414 days, the present was a minefield. It was uncertain which days I would step on and detonate the bomb of some past misdeed. We treaded carefully on the scorched earth of memory and forgiveness. Nothing felt more tenuous than my grip on what had happened and nothing more fragile than rebuilding what I had destroyed.

I know that somewhere in the middle of the Great Unpleasantness, I tried to find recovery. There were days, sometimes weeks, a month here or there, where I would claw my way through detox and stop the madness. But these attempts only seemed to make things worse. One time, three friends came to my door to conduct some kind of intervention. It was a disaster. I had been kicking for two days. Shameful and embarrassed after they left, I immediately bought a bottle. I love them fiercely for what they tried to do, but there was nothing they could do. The baffling irony of addiction is that you can recover only if you want to. Forcing compliance doesn't work. It inspires retaliation and usually still more relapse. This is why rehabs and jails almost always don't work. And yet, addiction itself keeps the addict enslaved, unable to want to stop. I am still in awe that I was granted that tiny window somewhere along the line and, even more baffling, that I slipped through it.

I did accomplish one period of sobriety during the yearlong relapse that lasted 117 days. I know this exactly because the documents I collected, ordered, read, and eventually filed away clearly revealed the day I quit drinking and the day I started up again.

I remember some of this clean time, too, though even without drugs and alcohol in my system, my memory was dwarfed by shadows, the brain festering and pickled. I do know that during that time, the house was clean, the dog was walked, breakfast was served, laundry washed and folded. There was furtive hope. I can still remember the way they watched me, from the corner of their eyes, treading lightly in their optimism.

I know this time because, on April 9, during this clean time, I read an article in the *Los Angeles Times* about an automobile-related death of a police officer. He had been killed four days earlier after a woman ran her car into him, gruesomely pinning him to the car in front of him. He was rushed to the hospital, put on life support for a few days, and then he died.

The driver's name was Qaneak Shaney Cobb. She was thirty-three years old and had a few drug-related and theft convictions behind her. She was arrested on DUI and possession of narcotics. The following day she pleaded not guilty to one felony count each of attempted murder and gross vehicular manslaughter for hitting and injuring the officer. When he died, she was charged with second-degree murder. Ironically, the officer, Chris Cortijo, had dedicated his life to putting drunk drivers behind bars. During his twenty-six years on the force, he had made more than three hundred DUI arrests, the last one moments before Cobb ran into him.

I didn't have to know too much about her to understand that Qaneak Cobb and I had nothing socially or culturally in common. But we shared one essential similarity: our addiction. She was fifteen years younger than me, black, and had been incarcerated numerous times. She had a DUI that had turned into a murder charge, with years of priors. When I read the article, I had not yet had a DUI, and her story was a reminder that I had been, up till then, very lucky.

Yet I remember with absolute clarity that after I read the article, I became obsessed with her. For whatever the reason, I began to pray for Qaneak Cobb every day. I felt like I knew her, that I loved her. But I also think that what happened under the influence of her addiction scared me, and that maybe in some small way I was praying for myself, hoping that this would never be my story. She would not stop haunting me. You might say that for a while her story nipped at the heels of my tenuous recovery. I remember being grateful I hadn't killed anyone. And with that thought the word "yet" was the period at the end of that gratitude. I followed the case on television, on the Internet, in the papers. I wanted to know everything about her. I wanted to talk to her, to find her, to tell her that I commiserated with her. Most of all, I did not want to end up like her. I read the story as a warning.

The future did not exist. Before incarceration, I still erroneously believed, like only the free have the luxury to believe, that time marched only one way: ever forward. But those incarcerated by addiction, poverty, racial hatred, and jail know better. We know that history is the present, that the present predicts the future, and that time never marches only forward, but outward, backward, and sideways as well.

In the story about Qaneak, I also became obsessed with her victim and his family. Cortijo had children, an ex-wife, a life partner, and a plan for retirement. I was wrecked by the cruelty of his circumstances, that he would be killed by someone exactly like me. I felt the loss like it was my own. From all that I read about him, unlike the police who stepped on me and bruised my body, Cortijo seemed, in a city notorious for its scandalous police force, like a good cop, a great dad, husband, friend. A year or so later, I read many posts and comments from people once arrested by him, speaking to his kindness, and how his care was a major source forward on their journey to sobriety. It was a refreshing contrast to my experience and helped me along the way not to generalize about law enforcement just because my encounters involved abusive and violent cops.

I made a vow that I would go to Cortijo's funeral, but that I would also find Qaneak and tell her that I loved her and that I empathized with her. She was held on $1 million bail. She would likely do twenty-five to life because she'd made one stupid choice. How many times in my relapse had I drunk my way into a blackout only to turn the key in the ignition of my car? Hadn't I risked my daughter's life by putting her in the car and driving high on drink and drugs? That day, after reading Qaneak Cobb's story, I believed the future was mine. I would mend my ways. I would not do what she had done. Wasn't I better than all that?

But yet—I drank again before they buried Cortijo. And

again and again. I never made it to his funeral. I remained so tanked, I forgot all about Qaneak. Pandemonium ensued. Five months later, the siege would end, leaving behind an exploding debris field, littered with the corpses of memory and hope.

∞

There is a place in Russia called Tuva. The people there, the Tuvans, are famous for being throat singers. Throat singing is rooted in the sounds of nature. The singer produces a pitch and, simultaneously, one or more pitches over that. The Canadian throat singer Tanya Tagaq says you have to be willing to hang out with your dog and sound like him to learn how to sing that way. Throat singing involves in-breathing and out-breathing, as in yoga. The breath is about the life between what is about to happen and what just did. In Tuvan, the word for "future" (*song-gaar*) means literally "to go back" and the word for "the past" (*burungaar*) means to "go forward." Like its music, which is based on breath-making sound, the Tuvans' language is predicated on the idea that the past is ahead and the future behind.

One Hundred Years of Solitude similarly erases the boundaries of time. For the people of the fictional town of Macondo, time is a yielding door, a verb that allows for the fluid movement of befores and afters. And of course, master that he is, Márquez makes the contract with us from the very first sentence: "Many years later, as he faced the firing squad, Colonel Aureliano Buendia was to remember that distant afternoon when his father took him to discover ice."

Every storytelling tradition broken in a first sentence. Time is warped from the start. The end of the story is the beginning. Even the verb construction "was to remember" is a signal for readers to strap themselves in for the ride. And of course ice—cold, wet, relief—is magic in a land of sultry dense air, heat, trees, and thirst.

All the way through, Márquez forces the reader to move between the past, future, and present. Even at the end this is true, when one of the characters finds the history of his family as it was recorded on parchment "one hundred years ahead of time" by a gypsy. This old gypsy had "not put events in the order of man's conventional time, but had concentrated a century of daily episodes in such a way that they coexisted in one instant."

Such distortions of memory—you could even call them inventions of time—are so fluid that of course the magical, the hypnagogic, and the dreamlike are not only possible but commonplace, and therefore normal. Simply recapping the plot would be an injustice to the complexity and dynamic of *One Hundred Years of Solitude*. Like Ozeki's book, *One Hundred Years of Solitude* is about many things. Big themes: family, education and wisdom, the intersection of fate and free will, love, sex, and death. It's about the value of persistence, of never giving up in spite of the losses, a theme that appeals to me.

But it's also about the amazing details, myriad and memorable.

There's the woman who eats dirt, and the girl who is lifted into the sky by her laundry. The thunderstorm of yellow flowers and a plague of insomnia. I could relate to the latter; I was lucky if I slept more than three hours at a time in jail. One of the most powerful details was the rain that lasted for five years. There was one moment of eerie prescience that stopped me in my tracks: "'Science has eliminated distance,' Melquíades proclaimed. 'In a short time, man will be able to see what is happening in any place in the world without leaving his own house.'" This was published in 1967. *How did Márquez know?* His prediction from a world that barely had television sets was spooky.

And let's not also forget the long sentences. In one chapter, there is a sentence that goes on for *three pages.* This "uncontained, unchained torrent . . . like the monotonous drone of a guitar" is the anthem to womanhood and our suffering. It was not unfamiliar to me in terms of its depth or breadth given the women I met in jail. It seemed to me, in fact, that the greatest act of love that I could give was to listen to the similar cascade of rage and disappointment of my fellow inmates. It's an amazing sentence with 1,473 words, give or take. I counted it. Naturally.

As I read the book for the second time in Lynwood, I remembered how a few years earlier, I had read a mammoth biography on Gabriel García Márquez. One time, Márquez was on a bus when a deer walked on board. That, he explained, is where his magical realism, a genre that Márquez made famous, comes from. In an interview with William Kennedy published in the

Atlantic in 1973, Márquez told this story: "One day in Barcelona, my wife and I were asleep and the doorbell rings. I open the door and a man says to me, 'I came to fix the ironing cord.' My wife, from the bed, says, 'We don't have anything wrong with the iron here.' The man asks, 'Is this apartment two?' 'No,' I say, 'upstairs.' Later, my wife went to the iron and plugged it in and it burned up. This was a reversal. The man came before we knew it had to be fixed. This type of thing happens all the time."

For Márquez, "surrealism runs through the streets. Surrealism comes from the reality of Latin America." It is not something disguised as reality. The surreal *is* the reality.

That is why Americans, or anyone from a first-world country, can't write magical realism. Because our lives are too literal. Wealth, good fortune, and peace diminish our capacity to experience the magical. When something strange happens, we call it a "coincidence." We don't accept the surreal as a matter of course. Instead we dismiss it as a trick, an anomaly in our normally realistic perspectives. In the West, we measure phenomena; we put them in beakers and actuarial tables. We strip the miracle out of things.

Except in jail. This is where dogs roam free and lie on plusher beds than their human counterparts. Or where you can throw the apple seeds from your soggy, rotten apple into a Dixie cup and actually grow a tree from a bed of jail-issued toilet paper. Or where a pregnant angel appears out of nowhere to hand you, starved for reading material, a book that is exactly what you would have picked on your own. A place where a toothless drug dealer finds you underwear that's never been worn, and where the school-play Hitler steals your tree—you being possibly the only Jew in jail—only to return it with remorse and gratitude. It's in jail where twenty women of every color, wearing baggy XXL blues, contort themselves into yoga poses without self-consciousness, without cruelty, and with love in their hearts. Where birds appear and flutter in the Dayroom rafters. Or where a prostitute who calls herself Princess is dragged from her palace under the stairs and chained to a plastic chair.

Jail is the surreal land of the unbelievable becoming real. Like this:

The day before my release, I rise as usual, brush my teeth, brush my hair, put on my shoes, and head to typing class. I'm not sure how many words a minute I type, but in junior high school, while the boys took shop, we girls sat in front of typewriters and learned to type, preparing ourselves for our careers as secretaries. They were IBM Selectrics, and we typed the same thing over and over again: "The quick brown fox jumps over the lazy dog." The sentence is what's called a pangram. It contains all the letters of the alphabet. In the late 1800s, the *Boston Journal* claimed, perhaps coining the word "pangram," that the sentence is "A favorite copy set by writing teachers for their pupils."

Typing class, like everything else, had its comeuppance. I'm fairly sure they don't teach it in school anymore, since according to the latest scientific research, fetuses today are now already sending Instagram messages from the womb. In jail typing class, they use a computer program. After I turn on the computer, a vivid color screen comes up. The typing program is designed around what appears to be a vacation concept. You sign in with your booking number and start the practice.

Several exotic destinations—Australia, Bali, Paris—are depicted on the screen, each one representing an increasingly more difficult typing test. I click on the easiest, Australia, and begin typing. Fast. And freely. LaRue, sitting at my table, is, as usual, talking fast and loud about nothing. I type and type and type, trying in vain not to simply *ignore* her droning voice, but to make it go away.

There are 150 other women performing assorted typing functions or engaging in the various stages of sleep. At each table we have to share, among ten students, three computers. As I wait for my turn again, I notice a woman at the table next to me who has a book called *AA in Prison*.

At Lynwood the effort to bring recovery into jail is mostly hypothetical, so I was intrigued.

"Where did you get that book?" I ask.

"You want one?"

"Sure," I say.

She disappears for a minute. I watch her make her way to the "library," and in a minute, she returns with a copy of the book. It is brand-new. I am touched.

"Thanks," I say. "I've only been to one AA meeting since I've been here. But the deputies shut it down after about ten minutes."

"Classic jail mentality," she says.

The computer makes its way back to me. This time I choose Bali and begin to type my way through exotic beaches. The ladies at the table next to mine are watching me. They can't believe how fast I can type.

"Go on, girl," one of them says. Another calls the teacher over.

"Miss," she says, "look at her type."

Miss, the typing teacher, watches me type. I am in a zone. Typing straightens out my brain waves. With suspicion, Miss stops me and says, "What are you doing here?"

I am not sure what she means. Does she mean in jail generally or typing class specifically? I shrug.

"Here," she says. "Take this test."

She sets me up for a typing test and, no surprise, I test out of Typing IV or whatever the last section is.

"You can be my assistant," the teacher says.

"Okay," I say.

"Go around and help the others with their tests."

"Okay."

She leaves the table. I look at the woman who had given me the *AA in Prison* book. I say, "No way in hell I'm going to be her assistant."

The woman laughs.

There is an open seat next to her. Tired of LaRue and her incessant chatter, I figure I can move over to her table and pretend to be actively "helping" the teacher.

"Mind if I sit next to you?" I ask the woman with the book.

"No, c'mon." She smiles back. She has a beautiful smile and big brown eyes and the smoothest skin. Most of us suffer from the iron-rich, chlorine-infused water, which renders our skin dry and crackly. But hers looks young and supple. I want to ask her what her secret is.

"I am not going to teach you how to type," I say, using finger quotes around the word "teach."

She understands that there is no way I am going to lord over my fellow inmates by acting like a teacher to them. That would be gross. I sit next to the woman with the beautiful skin, and side by side with our matching books we exist peacefully in companionable silence.

"Thanks again for the book," I say after a while.

"Sure," she says.

Silence, then she asks, "What are you in for?"

"DUI," I say. "And battery of an officer."

She looks me up and down and says, "Battery? Little itty-bitty you? Good Lord, what did you do, beat him with your invisible baseball bat?"

I laugh. The other women at the table laugh, too. Everyone knows what we know. You don't have to explain bullshit in jail. At least not when it concerns the police and their version of reality.

"How about you?" I ask.

"I got a DUI, too," she says. "But I killed a po-lice."

That's when the chill of a lifetime runs through me.

"By any chance . . ." I say. Maybe it is the tone of my voice, but everyone else at the table stops to listen in on our conversation. Maybe it is suddenly quiet. Or maybe what I'm hearing is the loudest roar of the surreal I've ever heard. "Was he a motorcycle cop?"

"Yes," she says. Her eyes grow deep and curious.

"Did you smash him into another car?"

Her eyes open wide. "Yes, I did."

But I already know that she did. I already know who she is. My skin rises to gooseflesh. I remember my life. I see my past predicting this future, as time marks me down for the present right there, right now. Our matching books—the ones that brought us together—glow between us.

"Was his name Cortijo?" I ask.

She nods. "He had just made his three hundredth arrest for DUI before I hit him."

"You're Qaneak Cobb," I say.

"I am," she says.

Our table falls quiet. It is the clamor of stillness. The entire room has stalled; the women, their hands in midair, their faces locked into hope, madness, and sorrow, are bronzed into statuary. The only things moving are the birds in the rafters and the dog that wanders aimlessly, looking for freedom.

"I read about you," I say. "I prayed for you every day since the day of your accident. I wanted to find you. I was sober then. But

I don't know what happened. I drank again. I forgot about you. Till now. Till just now."

Tears pool in her eyes.

"Did you know that today is April 9th?" she asks.

Of course I know what day it is. I am a counter. I am married to my calendar. And I am leaving, if they don't forget me, the next day.

"He died a year ago today," she says.

"I read about you on that day," I say.

For only the third or fourth time since I began my sentence, I begin to cry. And then I feel the shut-down, unnavigated portion of my spirit flower. I touch the book she had given me. To be the recipient of the words she gave me in that little volume of helpfulness was the offering of benevolence, the gift of love. To borrow a line from Márquez, my bones "began to fill with words." To my surprise, everyone at the table began to cry, including Qaneak Cobb.

"You see how God is," one of the women says. "Mmm-hmm. Ain't no coincidences in this place."

There are no coincidences. I could ask myself over and over again, what possible chance was there that among a total of twenty-five hundred inmates, *I had sat next to—on my last day— the very woman* who had penetrated a drinking binge so deep that she was practically the only thing I remembered of it? What were the chances that this meeting would occur *exactly* a year to the date that I read about her?

Time had collapsed. On April 9, the year before when I had

read the story about the intersection of Qaneak's and Cortijo's lives, I didn't know that this moment, April 9, one year later, had already come to exist—a "reversal" in Márquez's terms—and was waiting for me here, in this place, on this day of my life.

Sitting there that day, I had jumped through the looking glass and the glass had shattered behind me. I would never return to old ideas, old ways of thinking, the old world that had enslaved me. The day I met Qaneak was the day I found my freedom. And at the last minute, too, of course. In less than twenty-four hours I would be asleep in my own bed.

As Márquez wrote far more eloquently than I would ever write, "Wherever they might be they always remember that the past was a lie, that memory has no return, that every spring gone by could never be recovered, and that the wildest and most tenacious love was an ephemeral truth in the end."

I no longer existed in time. Only in being. Only in love, and its impermanence. We took each other's hands. There is no measure of the distance we crossed.

"I will never leave you," I say.

And I don't. For more than two years, until she was transferred three hundred miles north to state prison, I visit her every two weeks. I help her out with money and books when I can, and once our friendship had grown, she learned to trust me enough to ask for the things she needed. But really, I can't calculate or quantify my love for her. Our love for each other crossed the usual boundaries and limitations of time and language. I love her vastly, in a way I've never loved another person.

CHAPTER NINE

Processing Out

You must love deeply. There will be pain. . . . You will lose
what you love and the more you have opened your heart the
more grief you will feel at the separation. But there can be no
real love without pain. Do not worry about the hurt. Look
past it. Open yourself to the wonder of every living thing.
Explode with love!
—Tolbert McCarroll, *Notes from the Song of Life*

About ten days before I was let out I had stopped going to the Pentecostal services. They were so unhinged and emotionally hairy for me. But on Maundy Thursday, I was popped from my cell for a special service involving the washing of the feet with the Catholics. I only vaguely remembered the term "Maundy Thursday" from my James Joyce days. I knew Good Friday was when Jesus was crucified. But I had to be reminded what Maundy Thursday was.

"It's when Jesus washed the feet of his apostles after the Last Supper," Rose told me as I sat down next to her.

That day there were about fifty of us sitting in a huge circle in the Dayroom. On the other side of me sat Nina, who was an opiate addict. We'd become close during the four days I was in Dayroom in the bunk next to hers. She often shared her journals with me, another uncommon act of trust. And we would talk for hours about what was inside the pages, and how much she hurt. Nina had lost everything to prescription medication and was inside on a felony for writing fake prescriptions for oxy. Her mother was dying and, in fact, would be dead the next day, Good Friday. Another victim of alcoholism. Sitting between Rose and Nina was like being surrounded by the jailhouse Holy Grail. Rose was a traditional Mexican Catholic, Nina a traditional Italian Catholic. They were earthy and pretty and spooky with their omens and superstitions and their love for the Virgin Mary and for baby Jesus.

It was the largest circle I'd seen in jail, comprised mainly of Latinas and white women. We waited in that circle for a while before the service started, so I borrowed someone's Bible to give myself a quick lesson on what Maundy Thursday was. It turns out that after Judas left to betray Jesus, Jesus wrapped a towel around his waist and filled a basin with water. Then he began to wash the feet of his disciples one by one. I wondered if that made them feel weird. Apparently Peter protested, but Jesus told him that if they didn't allow the foot washing, they could not be part of him.

"You also should wash one another's feet," he told them. "I have set an example that you should do as I have done for you. Very truly I tell you, no servant is greater than his master, nor is a messenger greater than the one who sent him. Now that you know these things, you will be blessed if you do them" (John 13:14–17).

It was a humbling idea. I couldn't picture the sheriffs thinking like this. Or anybody in power for that matter. But it blew my mind on a basic level. I wasn't shocked that *Jesus* would do such a thing. I mean, it wasn't surprising given not just who he was but who Christians made him out to be. But to accept something like that from another person, especially your superior in all ways, is definitely a confusing idea. It would take a lot of self-control not to wiggle while someone you respected washed your feet.

Finally, a very small lady in her fifties entered the circle carrying a tub, a couple gallon containers of water, some oil, and a few rolls of paper towels. She was tiny and had long, silky black hair. She wore simple white pants, a red shirt, and clogs. Two inmates volunteered to help her, carrying her supplies to the center of the circle. The woman spoke only Spanish as she read some Bible passages, speaking very softly and modestly. Even if I could have understood the Spanish, I wouldn't have been able to hear her because she was so soft-spoken. Everything about her emanated light and restfulness. In my entire time at Lynwood, I had not come into contact with a person like her, so humble as to appear almost meek, yet strong with her intention and conviction. Her expression was plain; I might even say it was sublime, without any appearance of self-righteousness or pity.

After the woman finished speaking, she kneeled in front of each inmate one by one to wash her feet. When she was finished drying her feet, she administered a few droplets of oil. At first the inmates were giggly and nervous and rowdy, like always. But within a few moments, the woman appeared so seraphic, so achingly saintly, that a hush fell over the room. You could feel the power of this gift, the devotional quality of her efforts, the absolute humility of her actions. All around me, my fellow inmates began to weep. It was one of the most unbelievable things I had ever seen in my life, and I felt myself softening in a way I may have never before.

When she had gone around the circle—it probably took an hour or more—she went to the center of the room again and bowed in front of us. Then, out of the blue, one of the hardest inmates in that place, someone who never spoke to anyone but who we all knew was on her third year in Lynwood waiting to be tried for the abuse and death of her own child, ventured forward. Her name was Helen. She spoke quietly to the woman who had just completed the foot washing. The woman nodded her head ever so gently and sat down, and Helen slid the woman's shoes off and gently placed her feet in the tub. She tenderly washed the woman's feet then dried them, after which she sprinkled oil on them.

It was in that moment—perhaps the most silent and still

moment of my life—that all my hope and all my fear, all that had hurt me and everything that had healed me, found its place in my heart. I had no judgment of self, no self-hatred, but no defensiveness nor overmuch self-love either. I openly wept.

The women beside me were crying, too. Everyone was. The pain and the suffering and the joy and the peace were brutal and glorious because they all came at once, seemingly unbidden. I held onto Nina, knowing her mom was dying. I held onto Rose, knowing her son was sick. They held onto me for what they knew of me, whatever it was they thought. It didn't matter. We all locked onto each other. We were one person. There were no differences between us. We had been crowned, it seemed, by light and by knowing. A wise rabbi once said, "There is nothing more whole than a broken heart."

I wish it could have lasted. But before we knew it, the deputies were shouting, "Back into your cells. Hurry up. Clean that mess up. Move it along, ladies. Goddammit, you're slow." So then it was over. But I won't forget that moment as long as I live. It didn't matter that I wasn't Catholic. In that room, love was just love. It was delivered by that soft voice of humility that shattered our hopelessness, acknowledged our pain, and gave us reprieve. After I was locked up inside my cell again, I watched the little, quiet lady leaving the dorm with the few paper towels she had left, her empty water jugs, her tub, and her bottles of oil. I could almost hear those oil bottles clinking together as she walked. I recalled then that day that seemed so long ago now when I had come out of my roaring detox in New Mexico and saw the crescent moon and the glittery stars and thought that if I were going to carry on and survive, I would have to learn how to love. And that's when I understood that when you truly love, you aren't conscious of it; it just arises out of the mist, halcyon and golden. I think of that mythical bird breeding in her nest that floats in the sea during winter solstice, charming the winds and waves into calm and peace. That was how I pictured the way love looked.

∞

On my last night, for the first time ever, I sleep like the dead. Of all my experiences in Lynwood, meeting Qaneak brought me to a presence that I can't define. A laying down of my sword, an opening for a new God.

At 4:30 a.m., I wake up to pee. Outside the Dayroom it is quiet. The brown light bathes the module. I can see the dog below in shadow looking out, its eyes lighted. I know that I am leaving. I am not afraid. I have lost all fear. As I pee, I hear the sound of boots on the steps to upper tier. I know he is coming for me. I don't even bother to cover myself. As I take my last piss in jail, the deputy says through the glass, "Schwartz, 531, roll up."

Tiffany is awake. She is smiling. "I'll write to you," she says.

"So long, girl," I say.

I roll up, taking my time. I give Tiffany my stamps, my

envelopes, my shower shoes, my commissary, which includes my vending card—there's never anything in the machines anyway, but she can have it—my shampoo, my baby oil, my toothpaste, my extra T-shirts, my flannels, my Keefe coffee, and my fireballs.

"Here's some pencils. Go to town on the fake-up," I say.

"Thanks."

"Hurry up," the deputy says.

"Cool your jets," I say. Then under my breath, "You asshole motherfucker."

He leaves the door open and stomps his way back down the stairs. I look at Tiffany. "He's gotta hurry back to his perch cuz it hurts for him to have to stand up," I say.

She laughs.

The only thing I take are my books, my letters, my apple tree, and all my writings, including my thinking reports, my EBI journal, my tests from school, my calendar, my handmade sixty-day recovery chip, and the poems that Tiffany and I spent time writing and sharing. The last book I pack is the one my friend Lisa Dee sent me. It's the weirdest book I've ever seen. It's called *Notes from the Song of Life: A Spiritual Companion*. The book was written by a former lawyer from Portland, Oregon, named Tolbert McCarroll, who became a lay monk of the Starcross Monastic Community, which probably most people have never heard about.

After his wife died in the late 1970s, McCarroll gave up his law practice and bought property in northern coastal Sonoma County, in the redwoods of California. There he established a retreat center and commune where they supported themselves by making and selling award-winning olive oil. McCarroll, known as Brother Toby, had bought the ramshackle property from the sale of a Victorian house he owned in San Francisco. He wanted to spend the rest of his life reading and in quiet contemplation. But that wasn't in the plans for him. When the AIDS pandemic hit, he and his fellow lay monks, Sister Marti Aggeler and Julie DeRossi, resolved to help the AIDS babies who were abandoned and isolated in US hospitals. He eventually became father to six AIDS babies. He once told a reporter, "There is absolutely nothing more contemplative as being with a child who is dying."

I hardly knew Lisa Dee, but my friends had given my booking number and address to people in my recovery community, so many of them sent me letters and books. Lisa had sent it from Amazon, along with a note: *Thinking of you, Sweet Leslie, sending warm hugs. Love, Lisa Dee.* When I saw her after I was released, she was fighting breast cancer. Then her father died. She was a pillar of strength. Once, I went to watch her sing in a gospel choir, but in her real life, she played in a punk rock band and worked a regular job. I am tied to her forever for this gift that came unasked for, surprising me, the pages holding me, as if they were her arms. And while I tried to find traces of crazy or cult in the book, I couldn't. I found only strength.

I turn to it in my last minutes before release and open it on a random page. "Check this out," I say, reading it to Tiffany.

The gateway to the spiritual path is you. . . . Within every self-absorbed person is a divine flame. It may take many years for the flame to be liberated, but it is there. No matter how hard it is to accept, you must under-stand that the only difference between you and any holy person you admire is that your hero has discovered her or his own nature.

"Nice," Tiffany says, yawning.

She's a millennial. She thinks she knows everything.

"See you on the outs," I say.

I will see her on the outs. Once. Then she will relapse and disappear.

I walk downstairs.

"Make your call," the deputy says.

I call Greg. "Come," I say.

Everyone is asleep. Denise sees me with my roll-up and my duffel that Duckie found for me a million years ago. She leaves her Dayroom bed and comes over to hug me.

"Godspeed," she says.

"See you," I say.

She doesn't cry. Her face is gaunt, skeletal. She looks devastated.

"Keep up the yoga," I say.

She walks back to her bunk, crawls in, and, in the darkness, fades from view. This is the hour they come for us and let us go home. But we can't leave till our ride gets here on account of the projects across the streets.

"Too many rapes and dismemberments while girls walked to the train station," a deputy said once. Was it me being paranoid, or did he sound disappointed about the mandated safety precautions? He probably found getting up and releasing people too much exertion for his corpulent body.

The thing about releasing us at 4:30 a.m. is that most people don't have rides at that hour, so they are returned to their dorm to be released at sunup instead. This way they can get raped and dismembered walking to the train station by daylight.

The deputy is about to take me back when all of a sudden Wolf Eyes appears.

"I'll take her," she says.

She's like the Witch of Buchenwald. She has some weird accent—maybe German or Eastern European. Her hair is fuzzy and buzz-cut and her eyes are bluish gray. She has no waist, and her body is sausage-like, stuffed into too-tight khakis. I remember her from Exit Dorm. She was constantly punishing us for being "too loud" or not tucking in our shirts. This way she didn't have to program us, which meant she didn't have to do any work. If she did program us, she'd give us fifteen minutes then lock us up. If anyone was still in the shower after fifteen minutes, she'd take program away from us the next day.

"Good morning," I say.

She glares at me. "Why are you talking to me? I didn't say you could talk to me."

"Fine, thanks, and you?" I say.

"Stop talking to me. I didn't give you permission to talk to me."

I try my hardest not to laugh at her. *Poor lady*, I think.

She marches me down several seemingly interminable hallways, up and down elevators. It's like a fucking maze. I don't know how they don't get lost, especially with such low average IQs.

When she dumps me off back where I started, she says, "See you back here again, real soon."

"You betcha," I say, giving her a thumbs-up.

Cunt.

They put me in a cell. I have to wait until they can confirm my ride and there's some trouble. Greg isn't picking up. I'm starting to panic. I call and call. All I can think is, *I am at peace because I choose to be at peace.* But this temporary snafu sets me back. I try to breathe. It catches, ragged. The image of me being escorted by Wolf Eyes back to my cell has lodged itself firmly into my well-being. Finally the deputy gets through to him. When I see him, I will kiss him. Then slug him.

Another woman arrives, another inmate being processed out. I compare processing in to processing out. The ratios in terms of numbers are comparable to birth and death rates. More come in than go out. I chew on that for a minute. The woman who arrives is very pretty, closer to my age, with a wide-open face and sparkly eyes. Eyes that are engaged in the world. Smart. The two of us know we are ancient relics in jail, but as such we get the most respect.

We are smiling. We both have rides. While we wait for our street clothes, we are transferred out of one holding cell into another holding cell. Inside my jail-issued duffel is my apple tree. I keep checking on it.

"I'm Serena," the woman says.

"Hey."

We exchange the usual Q&A: Why were you here, how long did you do, is this your release date or early? Then she says, "Every day, I was going to court with this bitch who was defending herself on a murder charge. She had all these legal books and legal pads. She killed her own mama."

"Damn," I say.

"She snitched on people. That was her thing. She put a lot of people in lockdown. That was one crazy bitch."

As she's telling me this, my mind is elsewhere. I am thinking about Starbucks and fresh fruit and pho and Thai food, and sitting at Happy Tom's eating huevos rancheros with my kid, and eating plain Greek yogurt and Extreme Moose Tracks with chocolate syrup, and sex, and sex, and sex, and no peanut butter, no mushy apples, no hard-boiled eggs, no bread, no dildo hot dogs, no bologna, no plastic bags, no sound of plastic being removed from processed food. I am imagining a life where no one talks about their vaginas at the dinner table.

"So one day, this bitch goes and puts a peanut butter and jelly sandwich in her pants. But she takes the plastic wrapping off on account of the noise it makes."

"Uh-huh." I wonder why she's smuggling PB&J *into* jail. That would be like smuggling more pain, suffering, and constipation in with her, when it already arrives daily in her plastic breakfast bag.

I spot the deputy from a long ways away, carrying our clothes in the plastic bags they were placed in after strip search that day forever ago. She is ever so slowly making her way to our holding cell.

"Schwartz," the deputy calls out. She throws my clothes at me. She checks my wristband, cuts it. For the first time since I surrendered, I am no longer 4261531.

"Get changed," the deputy says. She is all smiles. They are all smiles in receiving and releasing because that's where the feds hang out watching them.

Serena and I start changing. As she takes off her jail-issued underwear, baring her pussy for the world to see, she finishes the story. She tells me that the woman who'd killed her mom, and snitched on her cellmates, forgot about the open sandwich in her pants. She says, "So we get back to jail and we walk to our dorm and that bitch is saying, 'My pearly hurts. My pearly hurts.'"

I take off my blues, put on my underwear, my pants, my shirt, my coat, my socks, my shoes. Everything smells like me. Coconut lotion, shampoo. Fresh, sweet, wonderful.

Serena regales me with the story and I am suddenly exhausted from the diet of mundane and trivial gossip I've lived on for thirty-seven days. Evidently, the woman who killed her mom contracted some kind of burning, blistery infection from the peanut butter and jelly. I am dressed, waiting for them to let me out. I'm thinking how I ate that shit *every day*. If it could burn a vagina like that, no wonder my gut was on fire day in and day out.

I don't want to listen to Serena anymore. I don't want to talk about vaginas and infections and women who kill their mothers. I want to see my husband. I want to kiss my daughter. I want to sleep on a mattress and not a metal slab. I want so many things. The deputy is coming.

"Schwartz, your ride is here," she says. "See you back here again real soon."

They think they are *so funny*. I turn to Serena. "Good luck," I say. I notice that once again, but for the last time, I am first to leave a cell.

She's still laughing. "That stupid bitch," she says. "She got her pearly all burnt up by peanut butter and jelly. That's what she get for icing her mama."

A few days before my release, I had asked Greg while on our daily call if he could please bring me a peach when he picked me up. Peaches were my favorite fruit. I was salivating for a peach.

When I see him, we hug and kiss. He's real, it turns out. There's his body, his gorgeous smell, his ratty T-shirt, his black knit cap, the hair beneath it maybe just a little grayer and finer than before all this happened, and those blue eyes that genuinely still make me blush when he gazes at me that way. Those are his lips. That's his hand in mine.

Before we leave, I put money on Duckie's account. She will be leaving in a week, and I promised her (she didn't ask) that I would help her with her transition out. I have her children's phone numbers, and in a few days, I will call her daughter. I have Qaneak's booking number. Though I vow I will never go back to that place again, in two weeks I am back, visiting her, and I do so for two and a half more years until she is sentenced to fifteen years to life and transferred upstate to the California women's prison.

As for Wynell, I do see her once. She is eight months' pregnant, homeless, alone. She contacted me through Facebook. I let her sleep on my couch for a couple days. She tells me she wants to give birth out of state so she can have and keep her baby. If she has it here, she tells me, DCFS will take her daughter. I give her $150 for the bus ride, though in my heart of hearts, I know she isn't going to Vegas, that it's just her way of asking for money by pretending it's for the Greyhound. On the outside, she is different. Colder, sadder, rougher. We talk about Lynwood. She remembers the day I moved from Exit Dorm.

"That was a bad day," she says.

"Yeah, it was."

Her memory of things seems dampened. She looks exactly like someone who is eight months' pregnant, living without much in the way of shelter or medical help or healthy food, would look. When we say good-bye, she is crying hard.

"I love you," I say.

"I love you, too," she says.

Greg and I leave the jail. The air is real, with its briney ocean scent. The beach, I had forgotten, was only a few miles west the entire time. We get in the car. It is still filthy, as always. The sun is just peeking over the mountains. So I have confirmation that the sun still exists. So do the mountains for that matter. And on the dashboard is the peach. I am filled with so much joy it spills over into laughter.

"Oh my God, look at that peach," I say. I glance at him. I feel shy. He leans over, and my heart flips, like it always does. We kiss, and in that private moment where we linger, our breath, our eyes, our body, I find home.

"Hi," he says.

"Thanks for the peach," I say.

His smile is golden.

I look at the peach. I am torn. Should I eat it? Or should I find a way to preserve it and put it on my altar of precious things at home? Maybe, I think, it is not a good idea to taste too greed-ily of that bite of freedom.

What I don't know is this: three years later, my daughter will tell me about her friend's father, dying of alcoholism. He refuses to find recovery, she will say, because of the "God thing." Be-cause he doesn't want people to know he is sick with addiction. Because, even while he is jaundiced, turning yellow, he says he "has it under control." His pride, like all pride, is the most dan-gerous weapon on Earth. His will destroy him. I know this from personal experience.

I will tell her that most addicts would rather die than ad-mit they are sick, or get spiritually real about the emptiness within them. Most addicts would rather keep their secrets, be-lieving their disease is shameful, and use themselves up with substances than walk the hard road to freedom. I have been to enough funerals to know this.

"You almost went that way yourself," she says.

We will lie there on my daughter's bed, her head resting on my shoulder. Outside the sunlight sparkles through the giant eucalyptus trees and I smell the bracing, lemony scent of their leaves. My daughter will be more beautiful than ever, smart, athletic, and, notably, a kind and contemplative person. She will sing all the time, in the shower, in her room, while walk-ing the dog, or wandering around and staring, the way teenag-ers do, into the fridge. She will be, to my joy and Greg's, a happy kid.

"It's so weird, Mom," she will say that day, her eyes wandering to the trees, the light, the blue sky, "but I have the family that everyone wants. I am so lucky. I never thought I'd say this, but you're the only mom I'd ever want."

Now, though, I sit in the car with Greg. The jail is a monolith of concrete and wire and sorrow to my right. As I look at it, I fully reject then, and forever forward, its phony attempt to shame me, to try and tell me I am bad or somehow defective. I realize the world has it wrong. It is the jail, with its cruelty and false sense of power, and the jailers within, empowered by a culture of abuse, that is shameful. What I know, without anyone having to tell me, is that I am enough. I am a good and lovely woman.

"Get me the fuck out of here," I say, holding the aromatic peach to my nose. *I will save it*, I think. *No, I will eat it right fucking now.*

Breathe in, breathe out.

He zooms the car. We turn left. We enter the freeway, the one I saw every day and every night from my tiny window in the cell I shared with Tiffany. I head toward home, toward my daughter, my dog, my garden, my friends, my life.

Released.

Remember that every prison has a chapel. Travel through the corridors of your own dark stillness until you come to a little room. Inside that room is a tiny spark that never goes out. If you blow on the spark with your full attention you will be able to make a flame. Then light a torch. Examine the walls. See how fragile they are. Look at the face of the jailer.

You are the jailer.

—Tolbert McCarroll, *Notes from the Song of Life*

Acknowledgments

I handed my editors an infant; they made it a grown-up. Thank you to Becky Cole, for acquiring my story; Kathleen Napolitano, who reminded me all the time how much she loved it; and John Parsley, who is so smart and most assuredly brought this book to its best incarnation. Katie Zaborsky also placed her keen eye and brilliant objectivity directly on the page. Thank you all for your diligence and care.

Much gratitude for Elizabeth Kaplan, who probably never had to wait for a writer to get out of jail before the real work could begin. It should be stated unequivocally how trustworthy and supportive you are and how much I appreciate your wisdom, your business savvy, and your kindness.

My readers: Erika Hayasaki and Luba Dean, thank you both for the many years and massive patience. For reading and editing the bits and pieces here and there: Noel Alumit, Essie Chambers, Anna Vodicka, Hope Edelman, Leslie Lehr, and Greg

Littlewood. It takes time, and you gave that gift to me. I am indebted to you.

For time and space: Vermont Studio Center, Hypatia-in-the-Woods, and Playa at Summer Lake. (Thanks for the ice skates, Michael.)

Thank you, Anadel, for being there every single day for me, including while I struggled with these pages. Same goes for Kim, the Empress of Hugs. I also appreciate the people who would not allow me to let this book take over my life—Dennis: Happy Bob's Day, and thank you for my Sunday texts; and Kathryn McDaniel: your friendship always shines a light on our astonishing journey. Thank you for listening to my story.

Thanks to those people, places, and things that helped me deal with the pain—physical, emotional, and otherwise—especially while writing this book: Dr. Arek Jibillian—"gratitude" is too paltry a word; and "magic hands" Lisa Schwarz. Without you both, the pain of sitting to write this book would have been sheer hell. Thank you, Paul Langlotz, for talking me through the worst of it, but mostly for listening. Jewish Women's Theatre at the Braid gave me back my career, and because of Tropical, Pathfinders, and H.P., I was restored.

About the Author

Leslie Schwartz is the author of two novels, *Jumping the Green* and *Angels Crest*. Her books have been translated into thirteen languages, and *Angels Crest*, the movie, was released in 2011. Schwartz has an MFA in creative writing, is the recipient of many awards, grants, and fellowships, and has been teaching writing for more than twenty years. She lives in Los Angeles with her family.